How to Write a GREAT GREAT Children's Book

Robyn Opie Parnell

How to Write a Great Children's Book

© Robyn Opie Parnell. All rights reserved.

R&R Books Film Music

PO Box 485, Morphett Vale, SA 5162

info@rnrbooksfilmmusic.com.au

ISBN: 978 0-9751609-2-3

DEDICATION

To Spock and Buzz, now in doggy heaven.

CONTENTS

ACKNOWLEDGEMENTS

Eternal thanks go to my husband, Rob Parnell

ABOUT THE AUTHOR

People often ask me how I became an author and started writing for children. I'll try to keep my explanation brief because I know you're eager to get on with reading this book so you can write your own children's book.

For as long as I can remember I've been a reader. You'll probably hear that comment from a lot of writers. It makes sense that writers love books.

And I do. All kinds of books. I love the feel of them, smell of them and taste of them. Yes, I also love reading them. I love the stories, characters and escapism. I love the possibilities that books create in my mind.

I grew up in a country town. While I was living there, the cinema and drive-in theater closed down. I was involved in school sports and had many friends, but in my spare time I escaped into different worlds – books.

As a child, I never thought about the people who wrote the wonderful stories that kept me mesmerized for hours. I saw names on the covers, but that was it. I didn't recognize the names as people – just words.

Then one day, after moving to the big city, I sat in a classroom waiting while our English teacher returned our essays. I knew mine would have a big red **A** at the top of the page. My essays always did.

Sure enough, when the teacher returned my paper, there was the big red **A** again, but this time the teacher said to me, "You should be a writer."

I'm sure this comment was never meant to change my life. It was a light, off-hand remark made as the teacher moved away to the next student, but the words nearly knocked me off my chair.

Of course! I thought in shocked wonder. People write books. People like me. I could write a book. Couldn't I?

I was fifteen so anything was possible. I went home and wrote my first novel. Not in one afternoon, but over a period of a few months. The novel was a mystery similar to the Nancy Drew series.

No one has ever seen my first masterpiece (so I can call it a masterpiece), mainly because it was **very** similar to the Nancy Drew series, which I loved. I didn't know any better at the time. I hadn't heard of copyright or plagiarism. Now I have, and I don't want to go to jail!

Next, I wrote what I thought was a picture book. Well, the story was meant to include illustrations – lots of them. So I assumed I'd written a picture book and naturally I assumed a publisher would love it, because I did. So I sent my story off and waited for my picture book to be published. Instead, I received my first rejection letter. What was the publisher thinking? Were they crazy?

Then along came a job and boys. Actually, boys came first. My writing was put on hold as I had fun, fun, fun.

Eventually I got married and the fun stopped (just kidding). After being married for a while, I decided to pick up that old thing called writing and dust it off. After all, what else is there to do when you've been married for a few years?

What would I write? I had no idea. I was an adult and I'd left children's books behind.

I joined the local writers' center. I read articles on writing and learned that writing romance novels was a lucrative occupation. So I sat down and wrote my first romance.

Keeping the hero and heroine apart was easy, but when they got too close, and the atmosphere sizzled, I froze with embarrassment. I felt my mum looking over my shoulder. I saw her frown deepen as the hero and heroine became friendly. And my mum was miles away!

I couldn't let my mum read this stuff.

One evening, I attended a romance writers' meeting at the local writers' center. To my relief, I met several writers who wrote both romance and children's books.

Children's books! No sex. No mum looking over my shoulder. I knew what I had to do.

I began reading books on how to write for children and again, I was struck with embarrassment. Imagine sending a publisher a manuscript of around 2,500 words and calling it a picture book. The shame!

I realized the second story I wrote, that wonderful picture book, didn't fit the **rules**. It was too long, too wordy, too descriptive and too bad. No wonder the manuscript had been rejected. Was I crazy?

I knew I had a lot to learn. So I read every book I could find on writing for children. I completed courses on writing children's books, went to writers' groups and wrote, wrote, wrote.

Five years later, after many rejections, I finally received the most beautiful letter in the world, which said, "We'd like to publish…".

That was ten years ago. I now have more than 89 published titles and another 6 due for release this year. I feel a lot wiser, though I still believe I have more to learn. In my opinion, when we stop learning we die. I'll never stop learning so I'll never die.

It's a great thrill to see, touch, smell and read your own children's books. I'm sure that's no surprise. It's an even bigger thrill to visit schools and see the excited faces of the young readers. They love stories, characters and the endless possibilities. They hang on to my every word as I tell them where I get my ideas and introduce them to some of my characters.

I love being a writer. It's the best job in the world.

Over the years, I've met a lot of writers at meetings, seminars, conferences and other functions. In 2004, I met Rob Parnell, the inspiration behind the writers' website www.easywaytowrite.com. Shortly afterwards, Rob asked me if I'd be interested in authoring an e-book on how to write a great children's book.

Does chocolate taste fantastic? Is Johnny Depp the greatest pirate to ever live?

Of course!

I remember when I started writing for children I read every book on the subject. I also did three courses. The knowledge I gained was invaluable. If I hadn't taken these steps to learn about writing children's books I wouldn't be a multi-published author today. Seriously! I might still be writing picture books of around 2,500 words. The horror!

Learning how to write a great children's book is vital to success. You wouldn't fly a plane without first learning how, would you?

Whether you want to fly a plane or write a children's book, it's possible with the right knowledge and guidance.

I understand the importance of information and guidance from experienced, published writers. Today, I'm still a sponge, absorbing every drop from agents, publishers, editors and other writers. I love the idea of helping new writers and talking about my favorite subjects – writing and children's books.

I loved it so much I did it twice. Drum roll please!

Here it is – the updated 2013 version of How to Write a Great Children's Book. It is my sincerest wish to help you become a published writer if that is your dream. Don't worry, the information is all in this book. So sit down, relax, and enjoy.

Best regards and happy writing!

Robyn Opie Parnell

SECRETS OF SUCCESS

Action

Recent survey results indicate that 80% of Americans want to write a book. That's a huge number – a large percent of the population – the majority. So the question is: do 80% of Americans write a book?

No way!

Why not?

For one thing, I find it hard to believe that 80% of Americans could actually sit down to write a book. And you can't write a book if you don't try.

For many people, including the survey respondents, writing a book is a dream. They dream of sitting at a typewriter or computer – an image romanticized by TV and movies. They dream of the finished product. They dream of the fame. Or maybe they don't even go that far. Perhaps they don't dream at all.

The fact that you purchased this book shows that you're ahead of around 80% of people. You want to write a book. You want to learn how to do it. And you took action to make it happen. It became more than a thought or a box ticked in a survey.

This is your first secret to success.

You decided what you wanted – your goal. Then you took action that moved you toward your goal. (Well done!)

If you want something, you have to do something about it. You have to make it happen through action. No one else is going to do it for you and let's face it, your book won't materialize by itself.

Sounds simple, doesn't it? But a lot of people – 80% of Americans – want a particular result – to write a book – yet do nothing about it.

Positive thinking is great. More on this in the next section. However, positive thinking is not enough on its own. Positive thoughts need positive action.

You want to write a book. Then take the necessary action to make your goal a reality. You can do it!

Attitude

Your thoughts control your destiny. And the really exciting part – you control your thoughts. Therefore you control your destiny.

YOU » THOUGHTS » DESTINY

Is there any better news?

You are in the driver's seat, taking yourself wherever you want to go. Sure, there will be bumps and twists on your chosen path. That's life! But you choose how you respond to them.

YOU » RESPONSE » DESTINY

Here are four random thoughts –

"I'm a great writer."

"Every day I write 2,000 words of a brilliant novel for young adults."

"I'm wasting my time. I'm not good enough."

"I'll never be published."

It's obvious which of the above thoughts will help you fulfill your dream of being a writer and which ones will work against you. In other words, we can see which thoughts will move you towards your destiny of a published writer and which thoughts will take you in the opposite direction.

Think positive thoughts every day. Because your thoughts – what you tell yourself – become your reality.

It's true. Your thoughts become mental habits in the same way as you develop physical habits. Repetition.

You learned to walk by repeatedly getting up and trying to walk. You did this action often until you could walk. Then you kept on doing it.

Our thoughts work in a similar way.

Do you often complain about never having enough money? Guess what happens? You never have enough money.

Do you tell yourself that you're fat and can't lose weight? Surprise, surprise! You don't seem to be able to lose weight.

It's impossible to think something and do the opposite. The thought is in your mind. It's what you're telling yourself and responding to. Therefore it's what happens.

A few years ago, I remember thinking that I hadn't had a car accident for a long time – a decade or more. While I was driving along, I was thinking about how long it had been since my last car accident and I was pleased with myself. Until I had a car accident! No joke. I ran straight into the back of another car.

Why? Because I was thinking about an accident in my car. I was thinking about the time between my last accident and well, the next one. Pretty soon I had the answer.

If you want to be a published writer, you have to silence the doubts that can cause you to give up your dreams. And you need to speak to yourself in the present tense.

"I am a great writer."

"I will be a great writer."

I prefer to think I am a great writer now, thank you very much. "Will be" a great writer sometime in the future doesn't help me much.

You need to put a time frame on your positive thoughts.

"I will be published by the end of the year."

"I will be published."

The first thought has a deadline – a sense of urgency. It forces you to discover ways of making the goal happen and then ways of working towards it. The second thought is ho, hum, plenty of time. You can think about it later. Five years? Ten years? On your death-bed?

I have two favorite messages that I tell myself.

I'm constantly telling myself that I can come up with great ideas whenever I need them. Because I tell myself this, and truly believe it, it has never failed me. I always come up with more ideas than I need. I wish there were more hours in a day!

The second affirmation is that I will write at least 1,500 words today. When I tell myself this, I always write at least 1,500 words, often more. Sometimes the target is 2,500 words. It varies depending on what I want to achieve and what stage I'm at with a book. Sometimes the goal is to finish the first draft today.

You have to make the goals achievable. There's no point telling yourself that you're going to write 10,000 words today if that's impossible for you. Or that you're going to finish the first draft if you're only on page 10 of a 40,000 word novel.

You must believe in yourself. You must have faith that you can write and be published.

You must believe that you have time to write. Once you believe these things you'll find ways of making them happen.

Published writers believe:

> *in themselves*
> *in their talent and skill*
> *in their stories and characters*
> *in their ability to be published*

Believe and you will achieve!

Ambiance (Mood)

Writing comes from within us. It's our ideas, thoughts and feelings put down on paper (or saved to a computer). Obvious, right?

But what, perhaps, isn't so immediately obvious is how our physical self and mood affect our writing.

Before you write anything, relax. Breathe deeply. Get in the right mood.

Taking a few minutes to relax is different from procrastinating about getting down to work. Procrastination is about avoidance. What I'm suggesting here is preparation. After a few minutes of deep breathing and affirmations, you're ready to start work – in the right frame of mind. Your mind and body are relaxed and open to all the possibilities of fiction.

How you feel physically and mentally affects your writing.

Never sit down to write when you're feeling angry, frustrated, hurt, or any other negative emotion. It's difficult to concentrate on your work. And these feelings are too easily transferred to your writing with the result that your characters start doing things that don't fit them or the plot. The rhythmic flow of your writing may become stilted or hardened. Your plot could take a strange turn that makes no sense to anybody, especially you.

Or maybe writing will be extremely difficult and you'll end up frustrated and discouraged.

Don't let your emotions intrude on your writing. The story belongs to the characters. It has nothing to do with you, except as the story-writer of course.

Go for a walk, do some gardening or a relaxation technique. When you feel good about yourself and life, return to your desk. You control your thoughts, so snap out of it and have fun with your writing.

It's important that you have fun and enjoy yourself. Being excited about a project definitely helps too. Otherwise you may give up and never finish the story. You could find yourself doing dishes and cleaning toilets in preference to writing.

If you're not having a good time or find yourself doing other things to avoid writing, then put the story aside and try writing something else. You can always go back to the story when the time is right. Or do something to get you excited. Remember that you control your thoughts and therefore your feelings. You can create or fake enthusiasm.

You can't expect your reader to have fun and enjoy your story if you're not.

I've learned over the years that when I become ill my first symptom is usually that thick head feeling. My head feels like it's full of cotton wool, fog or marshmallow, and my thoughts don't seem to make it through this thick substance. Basically, I have trouble thinking and getting the right words on to my computer.

When I feel like this writing is difficult. Sometimes I begin to question my story, my talent and abilities. Doubts sneak in, instead of clear thinking.

Once I recognize I'm actually ill and not a terrible writer, I put my story aside until I'm feeling better. I do other related things, like read children's books, answer emails, research the market and so forth.

Writing when I'm sick doesn't help me. It is not a positive experience. It can be too hard with my thick head. So I return to a manuscript when I'm feeling better and writing is a pleasure again.

Your Work Ethic

Okay, so we all know that writing is hard work. Thank goodness. Otherwise everyone and their pet goldfish would be doing it. There would be too many books – unpublished books – because there would be many more writers and many more rejections from publishers.

More good news! There are ways of making writing easier.

Write every day. This gives you continuity with the story and characters.

Even if you only write for one hour a day, you're still in the story, relating to the characters, feeling the emotions and rhythm. You're getting a daily dose of the fictitious world, not just your real life. This is vital.

For example, if you only write on weekends, when you sit down at your computer it takes you a while to remember where you left off and get back into the feel of the story and characters. It's like meeting them for the first time or wondering what they've been up to while you've been away. There's some catching up to do. You have to read many pages of your manuscript and the temptation to edit stirs your fingers to action before you're even back in the story.

How much time is wasted trying to get back into your novel? And when you finally do, it's time to pack up. How frustrating!

The smooth flow of your story is at risk when you write in infrequent chunks. You may find your voice changes from one writing spurt to another. Your character may feel like a stranger and do things that are strange for the character. It's more likely that you'll inadvertently change the color of his/her hair or eyes.

So, the ideal is to work on your novel for 3 or 4 hours a day. I can hear some of you complaining that you don't have 3 or 4 hours. Sure, I understand. Been there, done that. Remember that what I'm telling you is coming from my own experience.

Okay, so do what you can, but do it every day. Get up an hour earlier, go to bed an hour later, write in your lunch break, on the train, change your job etc.

Even fifteen minutes or half an hour every day will help. You can find half an hour, right?

If you really want to be a writer you'll find time to write every day. There must be some minutes in your day or night. Surely you can survive on one less hour of sleep or get through life without a particular television show.

If you simply cannot find at least one hour a day to write, then I suggest that you evaluate your thinking. What thoughts are stopping you from committing to a career as a writer? What's holding you back?

Look at your thoughts one by one and ask if it's doubt holding you back.

Fear?

I bet that most of you are being betrayed by your thoughts and you are probably not even aware of it. Confront these thoughts, challenge them, and make them disappear. You can change a negative thought by replacing it with a better, more productive version of the thought.

Here's an example:

"I'm never going to finish this novel."

Let's say you're writing a novel for 10 to 14 year olds with a word length of approximately 25,000 words.

You wrote 1,000 words today. Well, at that rate you'll have the novel finished in 25 days. Okay, you want to spend some time editing it. Great!

Now you can change your thought to: "I'm going to finish my novel in less than two months!" That's approximately 60 days, no problem.

Challenge your negative thinking with reality. Negative thoughts are like monsters. They only have life if we believe in them.

Remember that it's your thoughts that control your destiny.

If you think of writing as a hobby, you'll fit it in around your other activities – whenever you have some spare time. What if you don't have spare time?

It's too easy to let your writing slip if you don't take it seriously.

However, if you think of writing as a job, necessary to pay the bills (even if you have another job), then you'll be more professional and have a better work ethic.

Treat writing as a profession. Be business-like. Get up every day, dress in appropriate office attire and go to work – your study or a nook in your bedroom, wherever. Your attitude to your writing affects your work ethic.

Congratulations! Now you're writing every day.

Some of you will be lucky enough to be able to pick the time when you write. Choose the time that works best for you and stick with it. Some people prefer to work early in the morning – like me – and others prefer to work late at night – sorry, I'm too tired. Do what works for you.

Some of you will have to fit your writing around work and family. You can still do what works for you. Make the decision, make the commitment and do it.

Writing is a habit – and we're creatures of habit. Once you're in the habit, you'll sit down and write without thinking about it. Trust me I know this is true from my own reality. I've been writing every day for years. I have the same pattern. I get up, dress, go to my computer, check emails, ignore them until later in the day, start writing and don't stop until 1 or 2 in the afternoon. This routine has become such a habit I find it almost impossible to do anything else. I don't want to do anything else!

Try writing a certain number of words a day. "I'm not stopping until I've written 2,000 words". I know this works from experience too because I've done it many times. Whether I choose 500 or 2,000 words I usually meet this goal – and then some. Our mind and thoughts are amazing!

Work hard and you will achieve your dreams – eventually. History shows that people who achieve success are those who are prepared to work hard and keep working. They stick to their dreams. They never give up.

Be disciplined. Yes, you can take time off. Every person needs time off to recharge their body and mind, and to allow their subconscious to ponder their plot and characters.

But, remember, your novel will not write itself. Thank goodness. I'd hate my novel to have all the fun!

Your Work Place

Having a comfortable place to work is extremely important. Having a place that is yours alone for your writing is ideal, but not essential.

You don't need an entire room, though again this is preferable. You need enough space for a desk and computer and all the necessary work related items – printer, books, notes, inspiring photos etc.

This is your work place. It should be neat, tidy and professional, as if it's your office in a posh billion dollar high-rise building. Your work place and its appearance reflect your mind. Remember that your attitude to your writing determines your success.

Other things to consider:

Is there enough light in the room? Position your desk to avoid glare on your computer screen. You don't want an excuse to stop working.

Is there enough fresh air? A stuffy environment can make you drowsy and reduce your ability to concentrate.

Is the room the right temperature? It's difficult to concentrate when you're too hot or too cold.

Is it quiet? Turn the telephone ringer off if you have to or switch on an answering machine.

Do you work better listening to your favorite singer, musician or mood music?

Do you need to sell the TV? You'd probably get a lot more writing done, not to mention other things.

If you're easily distracted by emails and web surfing, then make sure your Internet connect is in another room, far, far away.

Some people need to delete the games from their computers or not install them in the first place. Playing solitaire can be much more attractive than fixing plot problems.

If you've placed your desk in front of a window for plenty of light, but find you spend too much time looking out the window, seeing what fun the neighbors are having, while you're stuck inside working, then move your desk.

If you don't have the luxury of being home alone, close the door. You may have to negotiate with your family. Tell them that you prefer not to be disturbed while writing, hence the closed door. You only wish to be disturbed if someone needs to be rushed to the hospital or the house is on fire.

You can always promise to spend quality time with your family after your writing time. You could read them a story, go to the park, cuddle – whatever – but after you've finished writing. Everyone deserves time for themselves. In fact, psychologists say that we're better partners, parents and people if we spend time on ourselves and what we want to do. Don't feel guilty! You are actually helping your loved ones and being a good role model.

Back to your work place: set it up for the best results – getting as much writing done as possible.

CHILDREN'S BOOKS

Are Children's Books Right For You?

What do you think of children's books? How do you feel about them?

"Children's books are easy to write. Anyone can do it."

Well, that's definitely positive thinking. Or is it?

Hmmm. Sounds like a negative thought in disguise if you ask me.

And, seeing as I wrote this book and you paid good money for it, you did ask me.

Firstly, if you believe that children's books are easy to write then I wonder if you'll ever write to the best of your ability. It's possible that you won't try too hard or push yourself. You could settle on two drafts of your story when more are needed.

Why go to a lot of effort when it isn't necessary? Trust me a lot of effort is necessary in writing any book, not just children's fiction.

You need to read children's books, study them and learn as much as you can about the genre. This is a recommendation I'd pass on to anyone starting out in a writing career.

If you want to write crime, you need to read crime books, study them, complete courses on writing, and in particular writing crime novels, and practice writing your own crime stories.

There are no shortcuts in your apprenticeship as a writer just because you're writing for children.

Secondly, this lack of respect for children's books will show through your writing. Children are intelligent, perceptive little critters who can spot a fraud at a million paces.

If you don't believe in what you're writing then you can't expect your readers to believe in it either.

Never write down to children. Sure, you have to bear in mind the age of your audience, but make sure that you treat them as intelligent little human beings. Never condescend.

Thirdly, how will you feel when you receive those rejection letters from publishers? Trust me you will receive them. Every writer does, at least at the start of a career.

Will the rejections crush you and make you vow to never write another word?

After all, children's books are so easy to write! How could yours be rejected?

Writing is a very competitive business. You have to give your book the best possible chance of being published. Publishers receive an enormous number of submissions every year. Your submission must be your very best effort.

"Children's books are easy to write. Anyone can do it."

Perhaps what you're really saying is that children's books are much easier to write than adult novels?

Sorry, but that isn't the case. Children's books can be harder to write because there are more restrictions on the author. We'll delve more deeply into the restrictions later in this book. For now, some of the restrictions include word count, age of reader, subject matter, little or no description etc.

Children's books can look easy to write, but the reality is that authors spend a lot of time, many months (or years) and many drafts making their books (and writing) appear easy.

Over the years, I've heard people say that you should write what you like to read. Why? Because writing is hard work and time consuming. If you don't love what you're doing then it's likely that you won't want to do it, that you'll never finish.

So, do you like to read children's books?

The parents amongst you should have read children's books to your children. You could be doing it on a nightly basis as we speak or it may be some years since you've read to your little ones.

Would you pick up a children's book and, when your little ones aren't around, read it for your own pleasure? Do you enjoy the stories? Or is the activity of reading to your child or children what gives you satisfaction?

What do you read in your spare time? Romance? Thriller? Crime?

Why do you want to write children's fiction?

I love children's books. I read a lot of children's books. I have a passion for children's books. I rarely read a book for adults. I spend most of my reading time tucked up with a children's book because I prefer reading this genre. It's natural that I would prefer to write children's books, too.

For ten years, I've coordinated a writers' group for unpublished writers of children's books. My experience has shown me that some people have the misconception that writing a children's story is easy.

Typically, they have written a story or two for their own children who naturally love them, and the would-be authors want to have their stories published. To them it's the obvious next step. They come along to the writers' group, learn about the reality of publishing children's books and I never see or hear from them again. I assume they thought children's books were easy and therefore needed little effort from them. When they found out the truth, they immediately gave up.

Most of these people never stopped to learn a thing about writing for children. They wrote their stories and came to the writers' group to find out how to get these stories published. If only it were that simple . . .

The fact that you have purchased this book, and are taking the time to invest in your education, sets you apart from a lot of people.

Congratulations. You're on the right track.

Don't worry if you're starting to wonder whether children's books are right for you. This section is meant to get you thinking about your motivation and if perhaps another type of fiction is more suited to you. Keep reading and the answer should be clear by the end of this book.

Before I started writing for children I tried writing romance novels. I received a personal rejection letter from a well known publisher who requested to see more of my work, but my heart wasn't in it. That's no crime. I ignored this request and started writing children books.

It's weird. I'd rather write about a big, black, ugly cockroach (*Black Baron*, Walker Books 2008) than a tall, dark, handsome hero. I don't know what that means.

Even if you don't end up writing children's fiction there is a lot of valuable information in this book that applies to any genre. Expanding your horizons can't hurt. When we learn we grow. When we grow we improve.

Defining Children's Fiction

Simply put, a book is children's fiction if the main character is a child. There are always exceptions to the above statement. Authors of adult fiction occasionally feature child heroes in their novels. For example, Stephen King sometimes pens horror stories with children or young adults as the main characters. Generally speaking, though, a book is children's fiction if the main character is a child.

Adults usually read about adults. Children usually read about children.

When reading a book, readers like to connect with or relate to the main character. Readers like to identify with the character and even romanticize that they are the hero/heroine. This is why authors spend a lot of time trying to create believable, sympathetic characters.

When I was a teenager, I wanted to be Nancy Drew. In fact, I still wouldn't mind being Nancy Drew. She has so many fun adventures.

What is the age of your main character or characters? Let's say they are 14. How many adults do you know who are interested in reading a story about the problems of a 14 year old? None, I'd guess – unless you happen to know a children's author like me. Therefore the audience for a book about a 14 year old is most likely children between the ages of 10 and 14.

So, a book is children's fiction if the main character is a child and the reading audience is made up of children.

Now, to take this further, children like to read about children solving their own problems.

From an early age, most children seek independence, in small ways when they are very young to bigger assertions as they mature. If you're a parent you'll know what I mean about children pushing their boundaries. I remember pushing my boundaries. I remember them moving. And I remember them snapping back like a rubber band.

Ouch!

Children rebel against what they perceive as unfair restrictions. They don't want to read about the same restrictions in children's books. Who does? Remember that most people read to escape reality – everyday life. The same is true of children. Children read to escape their own lives and that can include wanting to get away from the adults around them. Here, we are talking about a desire for freedom, power, or maturity, not a dislike of adults.

In children's fiction, children like to read about children solving their own problems with only minor assistance from adults or, better still, no assistance from adults. In fact, it's quite common in children's fiction for adults to be absent. A good way to explain these absences is having parents go off to work.

At the very least, adults are kept in the background. They are minor characters.

For example, I have a novel about a boy, Rocky, who wants to find his dad. Rocky hasn't seen his dad in eight years and his mum refuses to discuss his father. Therefore Rocky is without adult support. He only has his friends, Matt and Emma, to help him. The trio set out on a quest to find Rocky's dad.

Rocky's mum is featured in the story. She's necessary as a catalyst that forces Rocky to take matters into his own hands and for the simple fact that children have adults in their lives. But she is a minor background character and she definitely doesn't help Rocky solve his problem or achieve his goal. To some extent, she's an added problem or obstacle.

It isn't always easy to find a way for children to solve their own problems with a minimum of adult interference. The answer isn't always obvious. But you need to construct the plot so that problem solving by the child is possible and the solution must seem plausible given the limited experience and restrictions of this child (and your target audience).

If you can't find a way for your main character to solve his or her problem then move on to another story. You can always return to the first one later.

A few years ago, I had a conversation with an editor at a children's publisher about this very subject. She rejected my story because the main character didn't solve her problem. It had happened by accident.

There's another reason why the main character needs to solve their problem; our main character is supposed to learn and grow from their experiences. This is sometimes referred to as "the hero's journey" and is part of the satisfaction a reader gains from reading your book. If the main character doesn't solve his or her problem, then how does he or she learn and grow?

The subject matter of a children's book must be something that children can relate to given their limited experience. Your story must be interesting to a child.

Types of Children's Books

In this section we'll look at the different types of children's books. Children's books are categorized into age groups and word lengths. If you write outside of these perimeters you'll find it difficult to get your story published, if not impossible.

For example, publishers don't want to see 2,500 word picture books for 3 year olds. Nor do they want to read 60,000 word junior novels (with some exceptions, like the Harry Potter novels - the exception that proves the rule).

Having said that, there is a lot of overlap between books for children aged 6 to 12. Therefore, the following information is a guide only. It's impossible to define each category absolutely. It's always best to visit a publisher's website to see what the publisher is producing for the various age groups. Ask them if in doubt.

Baby/Toddler Books

These books are designed for the youngest children – infants and toddlers. They are usually very simple stories or educational books to teach children their ABCs, colors, counting etc.

These books are very short and are often made from board or washable plastic. They include novelty interactive books, such as pop-ups, press, poke, unfold and lift-the-flaps.

Picture Books

Picture books are usually 32 pages, though in recent times some publishers have been producing 24 page picture books to reduce costs. The main audience is aged between 4 and 8 years. There are also picture books for older readers with longer, more complex stories and sophisticated illustrations, but these are less common.

The word length for picture books is a maximum of 1,000 words. However, I know of publishers who want picture books of no more than 600 words. The picture books for older readers are usually longer 1,500 words – even 2,000 words. It's best to look at publishers' guidelines before submitting.

Picture book plots are simple with one main character and a storyline that is familiar to children aged 4 to 8. Your audience must be able to relate to the story to be interested in it. The restrictive word length means that there is no room for subplots and little opportunity for character development.

These books are highly illustrated, with illustrations on every page or every other page. The illustrations are as important as the words. There's no need to describe in the text what is shown in the illustrations (more on this later).

Non-fiction picture books are usually aimed at schools and libraries. They have a much broader target audience, greater word lengths and more complex subject matter. There are fewer rules and restrictions with non-fiction picture books.

Easy Readers

Easy readers are also called beginner readers, early readers, easy-to-read and read-alone. These books are aimed at children who are starting to read on their own, approximately 5 to 8 year olds.

These books are still highly illustrated, usually with a color illustration on every page like a picture book, but they are designed to look more "grown up". They are smaller than picture books, more in line with novels, and are sometimes broken into short chapters, to give a child a sense of maturing as a reader.

Basically, the text of these books can stand alone without the illustrations (unlike picture books). The illustrations make the books look more accessible and attractive to new readers.

Easy readers use words that are familiar to children and simple grammar and sentence structure (short sentences). They can have as few as two to five sentences per page. The stories are told through action and dialogue, like grown up books.

The length varies from publisher to publisher. As a guide, though, work on 500 up-to 2,000 words. These books are often published as part of ongoing series.

Many of my books can be classified as easy readers, such as *Chick Catches Dinner*, *Teddy's Sticky Mess* and *Helga and the Ogre*.

Transition Books

Transition books are sometimes called early chapter books or storybooks and are targeted at ages 6 to 9. They are a step between easy readers and chapter books, giving emerging readers a chance to become more confident reading alone.

Transition books are usually illustrated with black and white illustrations every few pages. These books are longer than easy readers, but are still relatively simple in plot, grammar and sentence structure.

For example, my book *The Pony Game* is an early chapter book of 60 pages and approximately 2,500 words. *The Pony Game* is part of Lothian Books Giggles series. The story is enhanced by a black and white illustration on at least every second page.

Chapter Books

Chapter Books are usually written for children aged 7 to 10. These books are longer in length and, as the name suggests, always have chapters.

The plots can be more complex with more characters, but not too many as to confuse young readers. These books have short paragraphs, though sentences are usually longer and more challenging.

Black and white illustrations can often be found in chapter books. The pictures are less important and more likely to be sprinkled throughout the text.

I recently had a book accepted for publication *Crabby Cookson* that, at approximately 8,000 words, fits within this category. The story focuses on one main character, with half a dozen minor characters. The plot is more challenging than a transition book, but there's still only one storyline (no subplot).

Middle Grade Books

Middle grade or junior novels are intended for children aged 8 to 12.

The stories are more complex, usually with at least one subplot. The subplot can involve the main character, his/her family or one of the secondary characters.

The subject matter of middle grade novels is much broader because children of this age group have greater experiences to draw on when reading. They have been exposed to a lot through television. But there are still some limitations. It's best to avoid sex, drugs, abuse etc. Middle grade novels are longer in length, usually between 20,000 and 40,000 words. By this time, illustrations are no longer important to the appearance of the book because readers are more confident.

The manuscript, *Looking for Dad,* is a middle grade/junior novel of approximately 32,000 words. The manuscript features one main character and numerous minor characters. A sub-plot runs throughout the story that, at first, seems to involve the main character's friends. Eventually readers realize that the sub-plot includes the main character, too.

Young Adult

Young adult novels are for ages 12 and up. These books vary substantially in length, sophistication and subject matter, as there's a huge difference between the lower and the higher ends of this age group.

Young Adult novels usually range from 30,000 to 60,000 words.

The plot deals with the interests and problems of this age group.

Stories can now be written with a number of main characters, though one is usually the focal point of the story.

Hi Lo Books

This extra classification has come about for reluctant readers. These books are intended to get children reading and keep them reading.

These books are usually aimed at schools and libraries. They are full of action and dialogue, and can often be described as fast-paced and action-packed. Black and white illustrations again enhance the stories. My books *Our Secret Place, Backstage Betrayal, Eye of the Future,* and even *Black Baron,* have been promoted for older, reluctant readers.

Your Audience

The audience for children's books should be obvious. Dare I say it? Children.

However, this isn't strictly true for picture books (and, to a lesser degree, easy readers and early chapter books). The youngest section of our audience can't read. Therefore parents and grandparents can be considered our audience as well.

Adults buy and read picture books to the littlest ones. So a picture book should appeal equally to adults and children. But remember that the content can't be too sophisticated, given that these small children have limited experience of the world.

We could also take this a step further and say that teachers and librarians are our audience as well. Every year, schools and libraries buy many children's books.

But, for the most part, our audience is our young readers. Let's take a look at them.

Children in the 21st Century are sophisticated creatures. They have a lot more options and demands on their time. They also have a far greater life experience and, in many cases, better education than their parents did at the same age. Simply put, they are less naïve.

Children also have more available to them – toys, games, technology and opportunities – than we did (or maybe I'm just feeling old).

Think of the things a child can do with a minimum of fuss. There are a multitude of toys to keep them amused for hours. They can play sport or participate in other energetic activities such as ballet, kickboxing, Scouts, rollerblading etc. It isn't unusual for children to spend hours playing video/computer games or surfing the Internet. They like to hang out with friends and gather at shopping malls. It's impossible to ignore the impact TV has had on the average life, as well as videos and DVDs. And maybe, when there's nothing else to do, our audience can read.

That's our competition. It's pretty daunting.

Lucky for us there are still plenty of children who choose to read, plus parents and teachers who encourage reading.

Books are competing for the same audience as the abovementioned activities. Therefore books have to be just as good, if not better, than these activities.

This audience has been brainwashed by television. They are used to watching an entire story unfold in one hour – two hours at the most. TV programs and films are fast moving, action-packed, simply because the story is told in a short time frame. It takes a lot more time to read a *Harry Potter* novel than it does to watch the movie.

Nowadays, children are used to experiencing a lot of images and ideas occurring together and changing quickly. This is the prime difference between the younger generation and their parents' or grandparents' generations, and it influences what we can do in our writing.

To be competitive, children's books have to be fast moving and action-packed too. Today's children's books have more dialogue and lots of action, less description. In some books description is limited to the characters' movements. Authors are expected to start the story in the middle of the action and end every chapter with a page-turner.

Our audience has high expectations. Hopefully now you can see why you must write the best children's book that is in you. This means working hard on your story, editing, rewriting, until you are satisfied with the end result – or as satisfied as possible for a poor insecure writer.

If you currently read children's books then you'll know what I mean. If you don't read children's books then you'd better start now so you can become familiar with the fast-moving stories of today.

Looking at our audience, girls are more inclined to read than boys. Boys are often described as reluctant readers.

You can increase your chances of being published by writing stories that appeal to girls and boys. Including characters of both sexes in your novels is a good idea.

Testing your story on children works well, if done properly. Your own children, their friends and cousins are biased and will probably like your story simply because it's your story. Or they might be too polite (or scared) to tell you the truth.

You could offer your manuscript to a teacher to read in class. You could ask an acquaintance if his or her child would read your story for you. You don't want your relationship with your reader influencing their opinion of your work. Useful feedback has to be unbiased.

Education Vs. Trade

Basically, there are two types of traditional markets – education and trade.

Education

Educational books are published for the education market. They are used in schools to teach children to read and/or learn more about a subject.

One type of educational children's book is the (easy or early) reader. They are often leveled so a teacher can gauge a child's reading ability and know when he/she is ready to move up to the next level of slightly more complex books.

Another type of educational children's book is non-fiction. Hundreds of non-fiction books, on all sorts of topics, are found in school libraries.

The school market is huge and demanding. Educational publishers can print dozens of books per year for this market because schools are always looking for modern, quality resources. The opportunities to be published within the education market can be greater simply because of the increased volume of books being produced.

Educational magazines provide another opportunity for writers. These publications, many of which are produced monthly, need contributions that include non-fiction articles, fiction and poems.

I tell you this because it may be easier for you to start out in the education field. But I also recommend that you continue to target the trade market.

Trade

Trade is the term used to refer to bookshops and department stores. This is the market that sells to the general public.

Schools will also purchase many books that have been published for the trade market. It's also possible to find some education books, even leveled readers, in bookstores. This means that parents and grandparents can buy these books for the children in their lives to help them learn and grow.

It's often harder to break into the trade market because trade publishers produce fewer books per year. There are fewer opportunities. Publishers will often stick to their own authors who have proven sales records than take a chance on a new author.

The more you write and the more you submit, the more likely you are to be published. Having said that, you have to submit quality work. Publishers sometimes complain about the poor quality of writing or submissions (formatting and layout of manuscripts) they have to plough through to find one gem.

Do yourself a favor and only submit your best work, regardless of the market you're targeting.

CHARACTERS

A few points to consider about characters:

a)   Characters are the most important aspect of a children's book – of any book.

b)   Characters can stand alone without a story. A story cannot stand alone without characters.

c)   Characters control the twists and turns of a plot and the final resolution.

Believable Characters

Why does a writer need to create believable characters?

The most obvious answer – so a writer can produce a plot for a novel. A writer is passing on a character's story to readers. The only way for a writer to discover a character's story is to get to know that character.

We all have stories. We all follow our own plots in life. To discover another person's story you have to get to know him or her. When you know a person well you can anticipate their actions and reactions.

It's the same with fiction. When you know your characters well you can anticipate their actions and reactions. You'll know or be able to guess what they would do next.

How a person reacts to various situations depends on their background, personality, strengths and weaknesses.

For example, a strange dog runs up to you. You might greet this dog with an affectionate pat and a kind word. But what if you were bitten by a dog when you were a child and that experience left you fearful?

Your reaction to the strange dog might be one of frozen terror.

A person's history affects the way he/she responds to certain situations. And you, as the writer, should know how your character would react.

To discover a character's story, some writers complete a detailed biography of that character. They get to know that person – name, address, age, birth date, star sign, family, friends, pets, appearance, school, grade, strengths, weaknesses, likes, dislikes, habits, hobbies etc.

What are your character's motivating forces?

Motivation is critical when creating believable characters. What does your character want? Why? How will he/she achieve this goal? Is their motivation strong enough to overcome several obstacles? Is their motivation credible? What on earth is carrying him/her from the start of your novel to the end?

In my novel *Eye of the Future*, Karen is struggling to come to terms with inheriting her grandmother's psychic ability. One night, she wakes in the middle of a terrifying vision; her parents and brother are involved in a car accident! Karen does everything in her power to change the future. Her motivation is strong – saving her family – and keeps her pushing against numerous obstacles.

Many writers make the mistake of coming up with a plot and then sticking characters into the plot. The writer then has to move the characters from one point to the next until a resolution is reached. The characters are forced to do certain things because the plot dictates them, not because of who they are – their character traits. The result can be unbelievable characters and an unconvincing story.

The problem is that the story came first and the characters second. Is that scenario believable? Of course not! In real life you can't have a story first. Every story is about someone or something. The story came second and only because that someone or something already existed.

Eye of the Future is about a girl who inherited psychic abilities from her grandmother and as a consequence is trying to deal with them.

The character and her circumstances inspired this particular plot. She inspires many plots. The story could be anything that relates to a girl who inherited psychic abilities and is trying to deal with them.

Hence, the reason why writers can pen a series of books about one character. Once you know the character's background, personality, strengths and weaknesses, you can create many stories about this individual.

Harry Potter is a great character. Every one of the *Harry Potter* novels developed from his character – background, family, history, personality, strengths and weaknesses. The stories didn't come first. Harry did and then he inspired many plots.

Having seen J K Rowling interviewed, it's obvious that she cares about Harry and what happens to him – as do millions of readers around the world.

This "care" factor brings me to another major reason why a writer has to create believable characters. Because a writer's main goal is to elicit emotion.

You may think you're writing a story to entertain readers. Yes, but to entertain readers you must elicit emotion. At the very least, you have to make your readers care about your character and his/her story.

Your readers have to want your character to achieve his/her goal, or they'll probably stop reading your book. Let's face it readers have plenty of other things to do.

Therefore, you want your characters to be realistic and convincing so your readers can care about them. To care, your readers must first believe in your characters and then their stories.

You, the writer, must care about your characters. If you don't care about the characters how can you expect anyone else to care? If you don't care about the characters how can you expect to write a great novel?

How do you care about a character if you don't even know them? How do you care about a character if the plot came first?

As mentioned above, your reader likes to connect with or relate to your main character. A reader likes to identify with the character and even romanticize that he/she is the hero/heroine of your story.

The reader needs to be interested in your character. They need to care about your character's plight. Otherwise they'll watch television or play on the computer.

Character development makes a huge difference, even if you're writing about a cockroach.

Black Baron is the name of the cockroach and my novel. As usual I developed this story idea from the characters. I started with a boy who likes to race cockroaches. He's a normal boy, involved in his own life and activities, messy, sometimes forgetful and irresponsible, but he has a good heart. Enter the clean-freak parents who own a deli, deplore dirt and pests, and would be appalled if they knew their son kept "a dirty, stinking cockroach".

In my original outline, *Black Baron* was murdered near the end of the story by the "clean-freak" parents. Let's face it the thing is a cockroach. Kill the ******.

Hang on a minute. *Black Baron* isn't an ordinary cockroach. As I wrote the story, I added a few details about *Black Baron*, intending to depict the relationship between Jake and his cockroach. The character development of *Black Baron* was meant to make Jake more convincing.

Black Baron, respectfully known as the champ, has won 17 races in a row. He lives in a shoebox under Jake's bed. After each victory, Jake gives *Black Baron* a treat of a few potato crisps. *Black Baron* likes to hide in jacket pockets, which allows him to escape the first attempt on his life.

As I wrote and got to know *Black Baron*, I kind of got attached to him. Okay, so he's a cockroach, but he's still my character. I couldn't kill him. I had to change the ending so that my buddy, the little black crawling critter, could survive.

I'm such a softy when it comes to animals.

I believed in *Black Baron*. I cared about *Black Baron*. I haven't been able to kill a cockroach since. I created a believable character – in my eyes, anyway.

Black Baron has been getting good reviews and most of these reviews mention the characters and their relationships (as if they are real).

A character can be broken down into three aspects:

- *Physical – age, sex, appearance, disabilities.*

- *Personality – likes, dislikes, strengths, weaknesses, intelligence, all things emotional.*

- *Background – family, experiences, anything that has happened to him/her prior to your story.*

I'm a screenwriter (as well as an author), so I read successful scripts by experienced screenwriters to familiarize myself with the medium. Recently, I finished reading the screenplay of the 1980's film *The Karate Kid*. The writer definitely elicited emotion in me. I cared. Even though I've seen the movie several times, I had to read to the end of the script. I couldn't leave the main character, Daniel, until he achieved a happy resolution.

Why did I care so much about Daniel, the main character in *The Karate Kid?*

The writer did a great job in creating a believable, sympathetic character. The writer:

- *Introduced the character as soon as possible.*

- *Created sympathy for the character. I sympathized with Daniel's plight.*

He's just moved to a new town and all he wants is to go home again.

He is constantly injured and harassed by a group of bullies from his school.

- *Put the character in jeopardy. As above.*

- *Made the character likeable and funny. Daniel also has a great relationship with his mother.*

- *Gave the character flaws and foibles. By no means is Daniel perfect.*

- *Put the character in a familiar setting or situation. I think most of us know what it's like to move to a new town.*

You, too, can use some of the same techniques to create likeable, believable characters.

The Karate Kid works because of who Daniel is – his background, family, likes, personality etc. What happens in this story is inspired by Daniel. His history, situation, likes and dislikes, how he reacts and the things he does, all move the plot forward. You couldn't take the plot and insert any character, let's say *Mary Poppins*. The story would fail dismally. Daniel is the story.

More on Characters

I use a biography (as described in the previous section) to learn more about my main character. I use pictures to see my main character because he/she comes alive when I have an image of him/her.

People seem more real when we can visualize them.

Have you ever read a book after seeing the film adaptation? Aren't the characters easier to imagine when you know what they look like (the actors)? Don't they seem more real now they have a concrete appearance? I'm sure we all have a clear picture of *Harry Potter*. He is real, isn't he? I can see him in my mind right now.

Whenever I can, I collect second hand magazines. I go through them, looking for photos of possible characters. I cut the photos out and stick them in a scrapbook. When it's time to write a new story, I have a bunch of pictures ready for perusal. I usually find people amongst these glossies who resemble my main characters. Real people.

A character is revealed to the reader in several ways – appearance, action, dialogue and thoughts. We learned in the previous section that much of the character is defined by background, history, family, personality and so on.

When writing for children below the age of 8 it is best to keep the characters to a minimum – one to three characters. Given their limited experience and knowledge, it can be difficult for small children to keep track of the different characters and the story.

As your child reader matures you can introduce more characters, but don't overdo it. Even adults struggle if the cast of a novel is too large. I know I do.

To avoid confusion, it's a good idea to give your characters names that start with different letters and sound distinctive. For example, avoid using Steve and Scott or Nick and Mick in the same story.

Confusing the reader distracts them from the story and ejects them from your fictional world, therefore reducing their enjoyment and character identification. You never want to make life tough for your reader.

I've read novels where two of the characters' names start with the same letter, say C, and I've found myself getting a tad confused as to who's who and what's what.

Writers sometimes give their characters habits, like chewing their nails, to make them appear real and distinct from other characters.

In one of my novels, the main character is Troy and his best friend is Nick. Nick has a habit of playing with his fingers when he's nervous. This little detail is meant to make Nick seem like a real person, but it also allows Troy to see when something's not quite right with his mate.

As I've already mentioned, dialogue is another way of revealing character. A lot of people have habitual ways of speaking.

"Anyways," "like", "you know" are dropped into everyday speech with infuriating regularity. Sometimes writers strive to make their characters believable by giving them a favorite saying or word like "unbelievable" or "man". But you have to be careful not to overdo it. You don't want to irritate your reader and eject them from your fictional world. If a character's dialogue always includes "like" or "you know" it can become rather tedious and annoying.

A story usually has more than one character. Developing these minor characters is also important. However, minor characters need less fleshing out than main characters. They're in the story to assist or obstruct the main character.

Be careful that minor characters don't try to take over a story. If they do, then you need to revisit your original idea and outline. Maybe you're writing the wrong story or the right story from the wrong point of view.

Your readers must be able to distinguish between minor characters so they appear unique and easily identifiable. This is why giving them distinct names is important. Making them totally opposite in appearance or gender also helps keep minor characters clear in your readers' minds.

Looking for Dad involves the main character, Rocky, and his two friends, Matt and Emma. In other words, the plot involves two boys and a girl. Three boys might make the story and characters confusing for readers and me, as the writer. A girl adds uniqueness to the characters and increases the story's appeal by expanding my audience to include the female perspective.

Characters in children's fiction are usually the same age as the reader or one to two years older. For example a story about a 10 year old is usually aimed at readers aged between 7 and 10.

Hopefully you'll remember from my earlier description of children's books that child characters should be able to achieve their goals and resolve their conflicts without too much adult interference. Adults should never save the day and therefore remove the child's power and satisfaction. Children want to read about children and they want to see their peers win.

Point of View (or Viewpoint)

One of the first things a writer has to decide when embarking on a new novel is from whose point of view the story will be revealed – who is passing on or sharing the story. It's through this character's eyes that readers see the plot unfolding.

A note: I originally used the word "telling" in the above paragraph. I originally wrote "who is telling the story". Later in this book we'll be discussing the writers' mantra – "show, don't tell". Therefore I find the use of "storytelling" or "telling the story" to be a contradiction. As a writer, you should be "showing" the story, not "telling" it. You are not a storyteller, but a story-shower. More on this later. Now back to point of view.

Point of view determines the voice of your writing. In simple terms, voice is the way your words sound on the page and when you read the words you hear that "voice" in your head.

For example, imagine the voice of a wealthy snob and then the voice of a poor beggar and finally the voice of an evil villain. They all sound different, right? So if you're writing a story from the point of view of a wealthy snob, the voice would sound different to that of the poor beggar.

Voice is the way you write, the tone, and could be described as bright, friendly, witty, intelligent, and so on. This description is how I view my main character, Rocky, and his voice in my story *Looking for Dad*.

Children's stories are usually conveyed from the point of view of the main character. This person's perspective on what he/she sees and hears is being shared with readers, and the voice is influenced by his/her personality, background, strengths and weaknesses. This is one of the reasons you need to know your main character – so you know his/her voice.

Okay, so we're sharing the story from the main character's point of view. The next question is – are we getting the main character's story straight from the horse's mouth? Or are we hearing it via a narrator? This question brings us to the various types of point of view.

First Person

I should have taken Black Baron with me. I would have taken him with me if I'd known he was in danger. If only I'd kept my promise.

The above (brilliant) piece of writing is from my novel *Black Baron*.

This excerpt is an example of first person point of view.

In first person point of view, the story is narrated by one character who refers to himself as "I" throughout the story and "we" when including others. This is the "I" viewpoint where the character speaks directly to readers in his own words. The impression is created that the character is passing on his story to readers as if he wrote the novel.

(Please forgive me if I stop using he/she to cover both sexes. This attempt to be correct and not offend is starting to drive me crazy.)

First person viewpoint means a writer can easily convey information to readers because the main character is revealing the story, not an outside party, and therefore can share every inner thought, feeling and opinion. However, to know a character's every thought, feeling and opinion, a writer must know the fictional person well and hence the need for good character development.

First person point of view allows readers to get close to a character as they see everything in the story unfolding through this character's eyes. This closeness makes it easier to get readers to identify or sympathize with one character.

First person point of view can be past or present tense, though past tense is more common in children's fiction. Here is an example of both:

First Person, Past Tense from *Black Baron*:

I was grounded for a week. But that didn't bother me too much. My priority was saving the champ.

First Person, Present Tense from *Looking for Dad*:

My eyes focus and the jungle disappears. Instead I'm sitting in our car, an oval in front of me and a bunch of girls playing softball. I can't help the feeling of disappointment.

There are limitations to first person point of view.

The main character must be in every scene of the novel to pass on information to readers. Remember that the character is sharing this story and cannot share something if not involved or unaware of it. Therefore, readers can only know what the main character knows, thinks and feels.

In longer books for older children, you have to find creative ways of slipping in the main character's description. A character isn't likely to stop and describe his appearance while narrating his story.

People don't mention their appearances in real life, not under normal everyday circumstances anyway. A person might complain about one or two features, such as weight, height or hair, but not every physical attribute. Nor is it likely that one of the other fictional folk will describe the main character. A compliment might come once in a while, though we're discussing children here. And it's cliché to describe a character from a reflection in a mirror because it will still be the character describing himself. Who does that?

In the shorter books for younger children, the word count leaves little or no room for description so this limitation isn't a problem.

Jake is not described in *Black Baron*. However Rocky is in *Looking for Dad*. The difference is mainly to do with story. Jake's appearance isn't important whereas Rocky's resemblance to his dad is an element of the plot.

Thoughts, feelings and opinions of other characters can only be conveyed through dialogue. For most of us, it's impossible to know what other people are thinking and feeling unless they tell us. Characters are supposed to act like real people and therefore can't know information about other people without it being revealed to them through dialogue, a diary or video (for example).

Third Person:

Lucy put a saddle on her pony. Then she placed a bridle over his long nose. "Let's go for a ride, Beauty," she said. "Over the hills and far away."

The above excerpt, from chapter one of my book *The Pony Game*, is an example of third person point of view.

Third person point of view means a narrator is passing on the story to readers. In children's fiction, the story is usually told through the eyes of one character – the main character. The point of view is limited to one character and is therefore often referred to as third person limited.

Third person point of view uses the pronouns "he" and "she" and the plural "they" when referring to the characters.

As the story is being told from the main character's point of view, readers are only privy to that person's thoughts and feelings. Readers follow this character through the story.

Again, focusing on this single viewpoint allows you, the writer, to build a relationship between the main character and your readers, creating greater empathy and sympathy for your hero/heroine. However, the main reason for third person limited in children's books has more to do with the age of the audience, their reading ability and life experience. Including too many different point of view characters can confuse young readers.

There are limitations to third person point of view.

The narrator and reader can only guess at what the other characters are thinking and feeling, unless, of course, these characters tell us through dialogue.

When you are strictly using third person limited, the main character has to be in every scene, as with first person viewpoint, because the story is being filtered through this character's eyes, ears and other senses. The narrator is still, in a sense, the main character though using "she" and "he" creates some distance.

The Pony Game is third person limited. The story employs a narrator, but it's still Lucy's story and therefore every scene is as per her experience – how she sees and hears it. You, as the writer, should never intrude on the story. You should remain invisible. Editorial opinions or comments are unwelcome. They could eject readers from your fictional world and ruin enjoyment. You're still writing the character's story and every event should be described as if by that character.

Third Person Omniscient

The omniscient point of view is god-like, as if the narrator or writer is sitting above the story watching everything unfold. You can show readers what is happening in different locations without the main character being in any of these places. In other words, you can show your readers what the main character cannot see or hear. The main character doesn't have to be in every scene.

With omniscient point of view, you do not allow your readers to get inside one character. You allow readers to share the thoughts, feelings and experiences of every character. Readers can see the story unfolding through the eyes of all concerned.

The main problem with omniscient viewpoint is that it makes it harder for readers to identify with one character. The writer doesn't focus on developing a close relationship between readers and the main character as in first and third person viewpoint. The writer involves all characters with a more god-like equality.

When writing children's books, it's best to use first person or third person viewpoints. Omniscient point of view is less common in children's fiction because young children can find all of the characters with all of their thoughts and feelings confusing. Plus new writers tend to produce better work when using a limited viewpoint, increasing their chances of publication.

I've never used omniscient point of view because I prefer writing a book as if I'm the main character.

Generally speaking, genre fiction such as children's, romance, horror and thrillers are usually limited to first or third person. Omniscient viewpoint is more often seen in literary fiction.

Multiple Viewpoints

Children's books are usually written from one point of view – the main character's perspective. You'll find examples of well-written children's books that use multiple points of view, but, as I said, single viewpoint is most common.

When multiple points of view are employed in children's fiction, the viewpoints are usually limited to two characters. Readers are privy to the feelings and thoughts of both characters as they tell their story, the same story, from their different perspectives. Chapter breaks are the preferred technique used to indicate that the point of view has changed from one character to another.

Omniscient and multiple viewpoints are more likely to be found in Young Adult fiction, where almost anything goes. These readers are confident, often reading adult novels, and have greater world experience. There is some cross-over with YA and adult fiction. Publishers sometimes produce adult versions of YA novels, the main difference being the covers and marketing.

If you're a novice or emerging writer, you would be sensible to stick to one point of view until you have more experience in the craft of writing. New writers have enough to worry about, enough of a job ahead in completing first novels, without having to worry about changing viewpoints, too.

Also, a publisher is more likely to publish your first novel if it's written from a single point of view. Naturally it's best to give publishers what they want.

I read a lot of children's books and almost 100% are written from one character's point of view, either first or third person. Even books that appear to have two main characters are written from the point of view of one main, main character. The story is still conveyed form one person's point of view.

Dialogue

Dialogue is an important aspect of character. You can learn a lot about a person from the things she says and how she says them.

In real life, when we speak we use a lot of "errs" and "ums". We have a tendency to waffle and use too many words. We repeat ourselves and go off at tangents. Some people actually say a lot of rubbish. Not you or I, of course. And there are the fabulously exciting greetings such as:

"Hi, Sue."
"Hi, Jan. How are you?"
"Great. And yourself?"
"Not bad. Busy."

Boring! Well, this dialogue might be okay if you are Sue or Jan. And it might be okay in real life, but not in fiction.

Dialogue in fiction is never a true reflection of real speech.

Real speech in a novel would slow the plot down. It would bore us. We would probably skip these parts or feel compelled to yell at the writer to get on with it. In keeping with our need for escapism, we're mostly interested in the exciting bits and want to forget the mundane. Real speech would be harder to read and at times irritating. We could put the book away and never finish the story.

I'm reminded of telephone conversations in TV and film. The dialogue is limited to what is important to the story. Rarely are there initial greetings, like the one between Sue and Jan. These conversations are straight to the point. And rarely do TV or film characters say goodbye or sign off in a polite real life manner. Hanging up the phone seems abrupt and rude, but is intended to keep viewers highly interested and focused. Listening to a minute long farewell would be boring and distracting. We would likely forget the content and purpose of the telephone conversation because the last thing in our mind is the farewell.

Therefore, writers use abbreviated speech in fiction that sounds like real speech, gives the impression of real speech, but is better.

Dialogue in fiction avoids all the boring bits. It's more concise, focused and clearer. It's what we would say if we had a chance to think about our words, write them down and edit them before we opened our mouths.

Can you imagine it!

"I want to yell at you. Can you wait a minute while I write down what I want to say?"

"Sure. Not a problem. I'll take the time to work out what I'm going to yell back at you."

Dialogue in fiction is not limited to a character's words. It includes spoken words and speech tags and actions and thoughts.

A speech tag is – he said, she said, he cried, he shouted, she called, they yelled etc.

Let's look at an example of dialogue.

This excerpt is from my novel *Black Baron*.

Turning around, Dad glared at me and held up his hand like a policeman

stopping traffic. (Action) *"I'm not sharing my house with a cockroach as if ... as if ..."* (Spoken words) *He flung his hands in the air, turned around and stormed off.* (Action)
Black Baron didn't take up much room, I thought. Besides, no one was using the space under my bed. (Thoughts) *"He's not hurting anyone,"* (Spoken words) *I tried again.* (Speech tag)
"It isn't natural," (Spoken words) *Dad said.* (Speech tag) *"People don't keep cockroaches as pets."* (Spoken words)

In this excerpt, the spoken words, speech tags, actions and thoughts work together to show how the characters are feeling and reacting. Even though we aren't privy to Dad's thoughts, we know he's angry because of his dialogue and actions. On the other hand, we have insight into Jake's thoughts and it's clear that he doesn't understand his dad's reaction. Obviously these two characters are at odds – the conflict is evident.

However, if you remove the actions and thoughts from the above scene, the dialogue alone conveys the conflict. You shouldn't use actions and thoughts to make sure your readers get the meaning of the dialogue. Doing this could be criticized as lazy writing. Good dialogue should be clear and easy to understand by itself.

Black Baron is first person point of view. The main character, Jake, is relating the story. Therefore, logically, Jake would let readers know how his dad is reacting and the physical actions are an important part of his story.

We often see physical reactions as more important than words. I'm sure you can remember times when you've told a story and you've been focused on describing someone's physical reactions more so than their words. You know the saying – actions speak louder than words. So, as writers, we include actions in our stories to add to believability, realism and interest.

Spoken words, actions, speech tags and thoughts work together to create images in readers' minds. Readers are able to "see" and "hear" what is happening in a similar way to how they "see" and "hear" scenes from the visual mediums of TV and film. The actions add to the realism, authenticity or completeness of a scene.

In the excerpt from *Black Baron*, Dad's anger is not just emotional. He feels it physically and responds with body language that shows he's angry, as if it's real life.

The above information on dialogue all relates to "show, don't tell."

Dialogue, actions and thoughts are used to "show" readers the events unfolding, as opposed to the narrator simply "telling' that this happened and then this and then this and so on. More on "show, don't tell" later in this book.

As we touched on earlier in this section, dialogue in fiction usually omits the mundane or unnecessary, such as greetings or farewells between characters. Speech in fiction is an improved version of everyday life and always serves a purpose.

Dialogue should always pass on new information to readers. It should do one of four things:

a)   *Reveal character and the characters' relationship to each other.*

b)   *Describe the setting.*

c)   *Develop the plot and conflict.*

d)   *Move the story forward.*

Good dialogue often does more than one thing at a time.

Let's look at examples of dialogue doing the above jobs.

a)   Reveal character and the characters' relationship to each other.

> *"Now it's time for me to go home," said Helga.*
> *"Not yet," said the ogre. "You'll go home when I say so."*

From my book *Helga and the Ogre*.

The Ogre's dialogue reveals his personality and the characters' relationship. The Ogre is a giant and behaves like a bully, forcing Helga to do as he says. The Ogre's dialogue also moves the plot forward. We know Helga wants to go home, but this option is being taken away from her by the Ogre.

b)   Describe the setting.

"It's not my fault your lawn joins your neighbor's lawn," Joe argued. "How was I supposed to know where your lawn stopped and the other lawn began? It all looked like the same lawn to me. The green stuff, you said."

From my novel *The Mad Mower*.

This example of dialogue conveys a little information about the setting. It's important to note here that the only description of setting included in this book (or any of my books) is what is necessary to the plot. This dialogue adds to character and conflict/obstacles, and moves the plot forward.

c)   Develop the plot and conflict.

"Have you ever thought of taking up painting?" Kelly asks Laura. Without waiting for an answer she adds, "Your singing's like garbage. It stinks!"

From my novel *Backstage Betrayal*.

In *Backstage Betrayal*, the main character Laura has problems with another girl named Kelly. This dialogue develops the plot and conflict. It also adds to Kelly's character and the relationship between these two characters.

d)   Move the story forward.

"I wonder if there are dinosaur bones in our garden," said Sam.
From my book Sam's Dinosaur Bone.

This line of dialogue moves the story forward because Sam immediately heads outside to dig for dinosaur bones. The dialogue links a scene in which Sam tells his parents about his trip to the museum and learning that dinosaur bones are dug up from the ground to the next scene where Sam begins searching for dinosaur bones in his garden.

You'll notice that I tend to use simple speech tags. "He said" and "she said" are nearly invisible to readers, as are "he asked" and "she asked". Therefore they don't distract readers from the story. These normal everyday words are still the best alternatives for speech tags. Creative speech tags, such as he hollered or he admonished or he mocked stand out and when used with great frequency can become annoying.

Years ago, I began reading a children's book that didn't have one "said" in it. I assume the writer had decided to avoid "said" and use creative alternatives. Unfortunately, all of these creative alternatives got on my nerves. I forgot the story and characters, and couldn't identify or sympathize, because I felt overwhelmed by the often ridiculous speech tags. As a consequence, I stopped reading the book.

Creative alternatives to "he said" and "she said" should be kept to a minimum. I do use alternatives that seem right for the scene, such as "she cried" or "he suggested". These words are fairly ordinary and familiar to young readers. They are sprinkled amongst the more common "said".

The easiest way to avoid the repetitive use of "said" is to avoid using speech tags every time someone speaks. You can intersperse speech tags with action and thoughts to show who is speaking.

For example,

Mum's eyebrows shot up again, like they were spring-loaded. "Do you know something about that horrid thing?"

I sighed and my shoulders sagged beneath the weight of my confession. "His name is Black Baron—"

From my novel *Black Baron*.

In the context of the story it's obvious who is speaking in this exchange between two people – Mum in the first instance, the main character in the second. Actions have replaced speech tags.

Basically, variety is the spice of life. You can vary your text – and your story – with a combination of speech tags, thoughts and actions. Don't stick to one or the other. Use all the tools you have and mix them for diversity.

When writing for older readers, you don't have to include speech tags, thoughts or actions with every line of dialogue. You can even write a short exchange between two characters without any speech tags, thoughts or actions, as long as who is speaking is clear. Omitting speech tags during arguments can add to the drama and tension.

For example,

"I saw him." *I touch my head.* "He has curly brown hair like me."
Matt raises his arms. "So do thousands of people."
"Yeah. Then why is he spying on me?"
"Who said he is?"
"He followed us to the park. Why would he do that?"
"Who knows? You're probably imagining it."

From my manuscript *Looking for Dad*.

Once I've established that this conversation is taking place between my main character, Rocky, and his best mate, Matt, I can drop all speech tags and actions to increase the drama and show the brewing of an argument.

Personally, I would only write four short lines of dialogue without speech tags or actions because any more might confuse readers and actually reduce the drama. Any time a reader has to re-read a sentence or stop to ponder some detail, like who is speaking, their escapism is ruined and therefore their enjoyment.

When writing for very young children, all dialogue is usually accompanied by speech tags or actions. Remember that younger readers are learning a new skill and have limited experience. Younger readers need more assistance – and clarity – with who is speaking. It's common in easy readers to include a speech tag or action with all dialogue.

Dialogue in fiction is like conversation in real life, in that it goes back and forth between characters. One person has their say and someone else usually responds. In fiction, every time the speaker changes, their dialogue is treated like a new paragraph and indented. Paragraph breaks are used to show that a different person is speaking.

In the last two examples, from *Black Baron* and *Looking for Dad*, you'll see how the characters' dialogue is separated and indented like new paragraphs. Mum's actions and dialogue are contained in one paragraph. When the speaker changes to Jake, I start a new paragraph that separates his actions and dialogue. This format makes it easy for readers to see who is doing and saying what. This is the standard in publishing.

Dialogue is always contained within quotation marks (inverted commas.)

IDEAS

Finding an Idea

Ideas are everywhere. They're around us every minute of the day. They're in conversations, television, observations, real life experiences, jokes, books, magazines, newspapers, schools, pets, hobbies, friends, memories etc.

One of the most frequently asked questions of writers is – where do you get your ideas? So I think the easiest way to explain ideas is to give you some background on what inspired me to write my books – well, at least some of them.

Black Baron began with a desire to write a book for boys. I love writing fast-paced, action-packed, amusing stories for boys. I didn't have an idea so I sat down and thought about the things that interest boys. Some of the subjects I came up with included sport, vehicles, pets, dinosaurs and bugs (just to name a few). At the time bugs interested me the most. If I was going to sit down and write a story over several months I had to be interested in the subject, too.

Next, I had to decide on what type of bug. I wanted my story to be different and original so I brainstormed varieties of bugs and dismissed many as being too common. That's when I came up with the idea of writing about a boy who races cockroaches. From there, I developed the characters of Jake and his family. I wondered what a boy who races cockroaches would be like and Jake came into being. Then I thought about his family and home situation, followed by his friends. The plot rose from the characters.

The Pony Game was inspired by my non-fiction book called *Looking After a Pony*. I'd contacted a local riding club for assistance with the photos for the non-fiction book and met a nice lady who was a wonderful help. Her love of horses got me thinking and reminded me of my childhood.

When I was growing up in the country, my best friend was horse-mad (in a good way of course). I'd call myself dog-mad. My memories inspired *The Pony Game*. I used to pretend my dog was a horse and try to ride him. I don't think this experience is uncommon as I've seen other children do similar. The characters were already partly formed – my best-friend and myself from childhood. From these memories I developed *The Pony Game*. The setting is based on my childhood home, too.

My novel *Backstage Betrayal* came from my fear of going to the toilet at a cinema after the final screening for the night. This is rather embarrassing. I'd appreciate you keeping it to yourself.

Have you ever noticed that entering the foyer of a cinema, at the conclusion of the final screening for the night, is like entering a ghost town? The candy shops are closed, sections of the building are in darkness and there's rarely a staff member in sight. I imagined going to the bathroom and while I'm in the bathroom, the remaining staff finish for the night, lock up and go home, leaving me alone in a locked, dark building.

Yep, I know it's silly, but these feelings created a good story. The book gave me a chance to explore my fears through a fictional character, from the safe distance of daylight hours and my home computer.

Never be afraid to explore your fears and emotions in a story. Putting yourself into a story can give your novel extra sparkle and depth. After all, it is YOU that makes your novel appealing and different from others. It's you publishers are really interested in. In publisher guidelines, you may have seen the question – why did you write this book? Or, why are you the best person to write this book?

While writing *Backstage Betrayal*, I drew on everything I remembered about being alone in the dark. I recalled not being able to see and hearing unknown noises, and my imagination running away with unlikely scenarios that sometimes turned me cold. To take this a step further, I was the main character. In a sense, the story was happening to me.

I really enjoyed exploring my fear of being locked in a dark building in *Backstage Betrayal*, as well as the relationships between teenage girls. Girls are not always nice and yes, I know this from experience, too. I know what it's like to be hurt and betrayed by my peers. I drew on my own history, and from the feedback I've received from readers they appreciate my honesty and insight. A few girls have asked if I'm planning to write a sequel. Not at this stage. Sorry.

Our Secret Place is based on a true story told to me by my ex-husband. When he was a teenager, he used to meet his mates in an abandoned house in the Adelaide Hills. It was freezing in winter. So, every time the boys met, they built a fire in the old fireplace. One night, not satisfied with the heat from the fire, one of the boys added extra fuel in the form of gasoline. I'm sure you can imagine the scene. Gasoline, fire, and no more house. Only the shell remains today.

You have to be careful when you base a story on real life events. You need to sufficiently fictionalize the event so that no one recognizes it as their story and takes offense. The last thing you need is a lawsuit.

Also, truth can be stranger than fiction. A few years ago, a publisher rejected one of stories with the explanation that it lacked credibility. This is the first time I've heard this criticism and I had to laugh because the story was true – based on fact. It actually happened.

Have you ever opened a cupboard, seen a jar of honey, and wondered what it would be like to be honey? I have. I decided being honey would be great. I'd be sloppy, sticky, moist, warm etc. Oh, except for one thing – I'd get eaten. This is the idea that got me started on my novel *Mrs Twitch and the Small Black Box*.

Why is milk white? I think white is boring. Why can't milk be green?

Now that would be more interesting. But wouldn't green milk be Martian milk? Well, we do associate green with Martians. You know, little green men. These thoughts gave birth to my novel *Martian Milk*.

I'm curious about all things paranormal and psychic. So I explored my interest in psychic powers in my book *Eye of the Future*.

What if? What if? What if?

Writers need to wonder – what if?

Question everything around you. Be curious. Be a child.

After becoming motivated by an idea, I then had to look at the characters. I had to develop the characters for these ideas before I could plot the story. Any character won't fit into any story. I had an idea and then I had to ask – whose story is this? Who are the characters?

All of my ideas required specific characters, with specific backgrounds, experiences, motivations and conflicts. Not any character will do. The ideas might have come first, but they inspired the characters. Then the entire plot could be outlined from the initial idea and the developed characters. As discussed earlier, you need to know your characters before you can create a fully fledged plot.

Subject Matter

When we write children's books we must remember our audience. Obviously the subject matter must be appropriate for the age of our readers.

For example, a story that contains references to sex and alcohol would be suitable for young adults, but not junior primary or storybook readers.

Almost anything goes in young adult fiction. I say almost anything goes because books have been written for this age group that deal with subjects such as rape, alcoholism, abuse and incest.

However, if you are an unpublished children's writer, I recommend that you steer clear of these issues. Stick to safer subjects and you are more likely to see your books in print.

Publishers are prepared to take greater risks on existing authors who have proven sales records, won awards, critical acclaim etc. These authors are able to stretch the boundaries. The novice writer faces greater limitations.

Also, publishing, like everything else, goes in phases and fads. The more sensitive issues may be appropriate one month and then six months later are out of favor. Maybe publishers received too much negative feedback and have become more cautious for a while. This attitude will change again.

When writing for the younger audience, your subject matter must be something these children can relate to from their own personal experience. That doesn't mean a certain subject – let's say, losing a pet – has to be directly related to their own lives. But it does have to be something they're aware of from the world around them. Or at least can imagine from the world around them. Children can imagine racing cockroaches, disagreements with parents and trying to save an animal (*Black Baron*).

Write about things that are relevant to these age groups, things that they would care about.

While younger children have limited experience, a wealth of subject matter is still available to the children's writer. For example, family, friends, peer pressure, divorce, death, pets, sport, holidays, moving, school, computers, bullying, accidents, injury etc. These are subjects that most children have either experienced firsthand or through friends and family. TV shows and movies have also broadened their experiences.

Children are familiar with many emotions. For example, happiness, sadness, loss, insecurity, fear, anger, pride, vanity, love, hate, pain, possessiveness etc.

My novel *Mr Fix-it, Not!* is about a sister and brother and their experiences with a father who thinks he can repair any broken down household appliance. He never does. He always makes the appliances worse and more expensive to fix when he finally takes them to the professional repairman. Life is not too bad, though, until the father attempts to fix the loud speaker at school, in front of everyone. Instead of a working speaker, he creates a dangerous fire.

The story is really about familial relationships, accepting people for who they are and how parents can embarrass their children. I'm sure plenty of children can relate to these subjects.

The title of my novel *Caught in a Cyclone* says a lot about the subject. The story involves a young girl and her parents who take shelter in their home during a cyclone. Their main aim is survival.

Not all children have experienced such an event firsthand, but they're definitely aware of natural disasters from TV and newspapers, and the after-effects such as charitable appeals, relocation and rebuilding. Fear and loss are strong emotions in this story, feelings everyone can understand. A subplot focuses on the main character and her small dog that goes missing during the cyclone. Many people can relate to the emotions concerned with losing a pet. The cyclone heightens the problem and feelings.

Young children have experienced the feelings from *Caught in a Cyclone* – fear, uncertainty, insecurity, love and loss – even if they haven't experienced a cyclone. These emotions matter to readers and therefore they care about the character's plight. They want a happy, safe, secure resolution so they can feel happy, safe and secure themselves.

Okay, I can hear you asking about fantasy. How does your audience relate to your fantasy when this amazing world is outside their normal experiences?

Martian Milk is set in the future. Paul and his mother fly to the supermarket in a space car. They use a remote control flying shopping trolley. Amongst the shoppers are aliens from planets I made up. Paul is afraid of trying Martian milk. He's afraid of turning into a Martian.

The world I created is fantasy. However, there is some familiarity – family, shopping, supermarket, trolleys etc. Also, the emotions and goals of the characters are similar to children and parents in our real world. They have to be for readers to relate to and care about the characters.

Martian Milk deals with fear, independence, being normal and fitting in. They are themes that everyone can relate to and care about, usually from their own experiences. The world might be fantasy, but the situations and emotions are still common. What else can we write about? Normal situations and emotions are all we know, even if we transfer them to other fantasy worlds.

You readers transfer their experiences and feelings from the real world to your fantasy world. Let's face it, this is how you created the fantasy in the first place – from your experiences and understanding of this world.

The *Harry Potter* novels are fantasy and millions of people relate to them. Many of the situations and emotions in the novels are familiar – family, friends, school, wanting to fit in, finding identity, good versus evil and many more.

It's important to make your story relevant to your readers. You want them to care about your character and his plight. You want them to identify, sympathize and emphasize. Therefore, you need your readers to have seen or experienced something similar or, at the very least, be aware of these things.

Twist in the Tail

If you haven't heard the term "twist in the tail" what we're talking about here is a surprise (or unexpected) ending. You're writing a story and you get to the tail – the ending. Instead of making the tail what seems most likely to your readers, you create a twist. Basically, you got off in a different direction and surprise your readers.

I love to surprise my readers with unexpected endings.

A friend of mine recently read *Black Baron* and told me that she never expected the ending. It was a complete surprise and she loved it. My ending was more satisfying than what she thought would happen. The resolution seemed obvious too, after she read it of course.

Great! Why spoil a good story with a predictable ending?

I'm going to take a little time to explain how I work.

So, I'm going about my day, minding my own business, when something triggers an idea in my head. The idea is usually character-based, like a boy who races cockroaches or a lonely, insecure boy who dreams of being popular.

At this point, it's important for me to like the idea, see the potential and want to write about it. In a nutshell, I have to feel excited. Honestly, I'm always excited about my ideas for fiction. It's some of the non-fiction ones that often fail to inspire me.

If the idea is for a story of 1,000 words or less, I'll start working on it at the first available opportunity, but only after I've completed the story I'm already writing. I always finish a story. If I leave a story in favor of a new idea chances are the manuscript I was working on will remain incomplete forever. What a waste of time and energy!

So, my philosophy is, never start a new story until you've completed the one you're already writing.

However, if the idea is for a novel, I go about my business, as if the idea didn't jump into my head. Now it's time for my subconscious to get to work. My subconscious ponders the characters and their stories, and plots my novel for me while I wash dishes, walk the dogs, shower, vacuum, drive, rest, sleep etc.

I allow my subconscious to play with this new idea for a few weeks. Then I sit down and work on the character biographies and plot outline. As my subconscious has been working on this story for several weeks, I feel like I produce well-developed characters and a well-defined plot with zero work. In other words, I've been thinking about all the necessary ingredients for this new book while I've been doing other things and, when I finally sit down to write, my mind already has many of the details worked out for me. I guess you can say I do a lot of preparatory work in my head before I start the physical labor.

I usually know the ending of a story before I start writing – thanks to my subconscious. I feel like I need a map with a final point to aim for and achieve. If I don't know the ending, my direction, I'm afraid I might not get there. However, story outlines are fuzzy little creatures that are apt to change when one gets the desire to save champion racing cockroaches from certain death.

Not all endings are equal. Don't settle for what appears to be a satisfactory happy ending. Think about ways of altering the ending to make it happy and rewarding yet unexpected.

An important note here is that stories for children under the age of 13 usually have happy endings. These children need a sense of safety and security. As writers, we allow them to live with the illusion that all ends well in life. Remember that they're reading for escapism. The fact that everything can be resolved, leaving no loose ends or unanswered questions, and everyone lives happily ever after is part of this escapism. The real world doesn't work in the same way – alas.

When you're writing for young adults, it's reasonable to have a sad or ambiguous ending. Young adults have more life experience, though still somewhat limited, and realize that every situation does not end happily. If they have ever been in love, they will definitely know!

My book, *Down the Well*, features a group of farm animals who, one by one, yell down a well. Each time, the animal in question hears an answering voice, repeating their own words. The voice sounds like a hen, then a cow, then a duck and finally a dog. The farm animals worry that someone – a hen, cow, duck or dog – has fallen down the well and try to rescue this poor soul by sending down a bucket.

The obvious ending – the animals are hearing their own echoes and no animal has actually fallen down the well. Yep. Great. Not a problem.

Okay, the animals might be hearing their own echoes, but my ending is different. A grumpy frog rises in the bucket to complain about all the yelling which is disturbing his nap.

Show, Don't Tell

Nowadays, a book or course on writing is only complete if the contents include the writers' mantra "show, don't tell" – a subject that is vital for modern day writers. In fact, this is such an important aspect of writing I wrote an entire e-book on "show, don't tell", details of which you can find at the end of my Articles E-book. I easily filled in excess of one hundred pages with information, explanations and examples of "show, don't tell".

Therefore I can only touch the surface here.

Let me make this clear – "show, don't tell" can be the difference between a rejection and a contract to publish your book. From recent experience, I can assure you that "show, don't tell" can be the difference between a story that wins a contest and one that doesn't.

Telling is a common trap that many writers fall into during the writing of a story. For a lot of new writers "show, don't tell" is a concept they have never before encountered. Novice writers often believe their role as a writer is to tell a story. Sure, you are telling a story, but the way you tell your story makes a huge difference to readers' experience, satisfaction, escapism and enjoyment of your book.

As I mentioned earlier, I don't like talking in terms of storytelling or telling a story because, strictly speaking, the last thing you want to do is tell your story. In my opinion, the idea of storytelling is a contradiction when you start learning about "show, don't tell".

So, what is "show, don't tell"?

This is telling – *She felt tired.*

This is showing – *She fell into a chair. Her feet ached and she thought about removing her shoes, but she couldn't muster the energy.*

Let me show you what I mean by "show, don't tell" by considering the visual arts of making movies.

Imagine you're a movie director and your job is to create compelling images on screen that draw your audience into a character's story. A movie director doesn't have the luxury of telling the audience that a character is scared. Words don't pop up on the screen for viewers to read – "Fred is scared". No, the director has to show the audience what is going on and he has no choice but to use visuals such as action, physical reactions, body language and/or dialogue. In other words, he must use things people can see and/or hear. Obviously a director uses images and sounds on a screen to invoke a prescribed response from the viewing audience – to elicit emotion.

As a writer, your job should be to create images on paper in a similar way as a director creates images on a screen so you, too, can elicit emotion.

A book, like a movie, is made up of scenes – or it should be – that involve visuals such as action, physical reactions, body language and dialogue. As a writer, you also have the opportunity to use introspection – the main character's thoughts.

To sum up here, the tools of showing are action, physical reactions, body language, dialogue and thoughts. If you are using a combination of these tools to write a scene then you are showing the scene. If you are not using these tools and simply writing prose – exposition or narrative – then you are telling your readers what is happening.

Showing is active. It's the technique a writer uses to make a reader see, hear, feel or smell – that is, experience – what is taking place in the story, as if the reader is a fly on the wall. Showing creates a bond between a reader and the scene/characters because the reader experiences everything that's happening, just as the main character does. Showing pulls a reader inside your story and lets the reader be the main character. It involves a reader by engaging his imagination and allowing him to participate by adding his own background, personalities and experiences to the scene.

For example, we all know what it's like to be scared. Therefore when we are shown a character being scared, we can add our own emotions, physical reactions and understanding to the scene.

Telling is passive. It keeps readers outside. Telling distances readers, makes them back away. There's nothing for readers to do or add because the author has done all the work for them. There's no interpretation. "Fred is scared". That's all, folks!

If you're aiming at scaring your readers telling your audience 'Fred was scared' doesn't cut it. This statement leaves no room for personal interpretation or improvisation. The imagination is uninvolved. But by showing that your character is scared through action and physical responses, you involve the imagination and allow your readers' minds free range to interpret the information.

Here are two more examples of telling:

- *He was worried.*

- *It was hot.*

What do these statements really mean? Who knows? Who cares?

Here are the same examples using show instead of tell:

- *He closed his eyes and rubbed his forehead. "Not today," he said, with a sigh. What was he going to do?*

- *His skin was coated with a layer of sweat and his clothes clung damply to his body. He glanced down at the panting bulldog sprawled out on the polished floorboards. Poor Brutus, he thought.*

Personally, I prefer the second showing examples. They are more entertaining because they get me involved in the scenes and characters. I start sympathizing and empathizing as I relate to the characters and how they feel/react. Been there, done that. I know how they feel.

And showing can provide readers with more information, subtly, without it appearing as if a writer is offering more information about a character or setting.

For example, we now know that the man, who is suffering from the heat, has a bulldog named Brutus and his room has polished floorboards. I could also describe his clothes as shorts and a T-shirt to add further detail.

And what if I changed the first example to – He closed his eyes and ran his fingers over his smooth bald head. "Not today," he said, with a sigh. What was he going to do?

Specifics, such as breed of dog, type of clothes or individual character traits, enhance the images readers can create in their minds.

Showing often does more than one thing. It adds to plot or conflict or characterization. It moves a story along. My showing version of "he was worried", featuring the bald man with the problem, does all of these things.

Let's look at it:

He closed his eyes and ran his fingers over his smooth bald head. (Adds to characterization by including description of the character's appearance and how he reacts to problems/conflict.) "Not today,' he said, with a sigh. What was he going to do? (Adds to plot and conflict, and moves the story forward, as the reader realizes there's a problem/conflict and, along with the character, wonders what he's going to do.)

Can you remember a time when you couldn't put a book down? The writer had you caught up in a story. She was showing you scenes that kept you hooked, with the use of actions, physical reactions, body language, thoughts and dialogue. Her characters seemed real and believable, as did the settings and plots. All because you were being shown enough detail for you to do the rest of the job – create real and believable images in your mind that actually kept you hooked.

Readers are less likely to become bored or distracted when they're involved in the story.

Look at your manuscript. Can you find statements like this – *"George was worried"*?

Delete those three words. This is an example of telling. You're telling readers that George was worried, rather than showing George's worry through actions, body language, thoughts and dialogue.

How can you get the message across that "George was worried"? How do you show it?

Think actions and body language that reveal someone is worried.

Here are a few suggestions –

George frowned and bit his bottom lip.

George clutched his hands to stop them trembling.

George took a deep breath.

You can also add to characterization when you show how a character is feeling and reacting.

Simone played with a loose strand of blonde hair that had escaped the confines of her ponytail. Twirling the strand around her slim finger, she wondered what to say to the teacher. She knew "I have no idea" was not the right answer to the math question.

The above is more effective than simply telling your readers that "Simone had no idea how to answer the math question". In the showing version, readers have to work out what's going on. Therefore, they're involved and participating. However, readers are given enough information to work out what's going on with a minimum effort. (Remember to never make life too hard for your readers.)

It's incredibly boring to have an entire novel-length story told to you. As readers, we want to see the action and hear the dialogue. We're escaping to another world. Why bother is there's nothing to experience for ourselves?

I recently acted as a judge for PM Moon Publishers' contest for new writers. The stories I loved, the ones I couldn't put down or brought tears to my eyes or got me attached to the characters, were all shown rather than told. The entries that I liked the least, the ones I found boring and couldn't care less, were all told. The authors told these stories. They were not from the main character's point of view.

Showing is about eliminating the writer from the story and making sure every detail comes from the main character's point of view. This gives the reader a chance to become the main character as a form of escapism. I have my suspicions that the reader doesn't want to become the writer sitting at home, hitting the keys of a computer.

Basically, when utilizing "show, don't tell" there is no writer, just the main character. As I mentioned earlier, when I'm writing a story I am the main character.

PLOT

Conflict

Now that you have a well-developed character – a person you know better than anyone else on the planet – it's time to write his or her story.

Your main character must experience some sort of conflict, which means the main character has a problem that needs resolving. Otherwise there is no story.

In my experience new writers sometimes get confused by what is considered a story in children's fiction. I have read some "stories" by new writers that have no conflict (problem). These "stories" might describe an event in a child's life, such as a visit to a farm, that is a pleasant time for all concerned. Perhaps this book could be published for babies because of the farm animals, though it would have to be very simple and short. Anyone else most likely wouldn't be interested or care. Why? Because nothing much happens.

Would you read a book about me going shopping? Of course not! Unless something interesting or out of the ordinary happened. In this example, my goal would be to go shopping. You don't care about my "story" if I manage to get what I want from the shops without a problem. You only care or become interested if an obstacle or conflict arises that prevents me from reaching my goal. For example, I arrive at the supermarket to find it open, but there is no one around. This mystery might intrigue you. Or I don't make it to the store because I encounter a spaceship on the way.

Therefore, it is the conflict (problem) your main character faces that keeps readers interested in your story. Readers want to know if the main character can solve his problem and how he will do it. They are curious about what is going to happen.

Bet you're not curious about me going shopping – unless something happens to make this outing unusual.

Let's go back to my example of arriving at the supermarket to find it open, but completely empty. This might be the start of an interesting story. But what if all the staff simply walked out of the staffroom and went back to work? Okay, maybe we're still a little curious about this strange event. The point here is that once you have created a conflict – in this case, the supermarket being open but empty – the problem can't be resolved too easily. Once the problem is solved we've reached the end of the story.

The basic premise of any children's book is that the main character has a problem to solve. This is the conflict. The main character attempts to solve the problem. She fails. She attempts to solve the problem. She fails. The problem usually gets worse or a resolution seems further away after every failed attempt. Again the character tries to solve her problem. This is the climax, where things get really bad or seem hopeless. Then, of course, things pick up and the main character achieves her goal or solves her problem. The final resolution is always happy in a children's book.

There are two types of conflict – external and internal.

External Conflict

External conflict is a problem that happens outside of the character or outside of the character's mind. In other words, the conflict is an external source that stands between the character and her goal. Often it looks like this conflict is out of the character's control.

External conflict could involve other people, animals, an empty supermarket, weather/natural disaster, lack of money, loss of a loved one etc.

As mentioned above, an external conflict must be something that cannot be resolved too easily or avoided. A character has to face the problem, with strong motivation leading them toward a worthwhile goal/resolution, or there is no story.

For example, my novel *Working Like a Dog* is about a girl named Lucia who badly wants new rollerblades. Her parents won't buy them for her and Lucia has no money. So how is she going to obtain her goal of owning new rollerblades?

This may seem like an inconsequential problem to you, but to a child it's a big deal. Remember your audience and think of the times a child has wanted something. They nag. They bug. They drive you crazy. They wear away at your defenses until you give in or lose your temper. They have strong motivation. Want. For children, want is enough, especially if they're influenced by peer pressure.

The problem in this story is outside of Lucia. She wants new rollerblades, but her parents and a lack of money prevent her from achieving her goal. This is external conflict.

Lucia decides to start a dog walking business to earn money so she can buy her own rollerblades. This is the solution to her problem and she is successful because she manages to gain five customers – five dogs to walk. Pretty soon she'll have enough money to buy those rollerblades. End of story.

No. Lucia strikes another problem. Walking five dogs every day is boring and takes too long. She solves this problem by walking all five dogs at once, but this leads to yet another problem. She loses two of the dogs when they fight with each other.

Again, this problem is outside of Lucia. It is external conflict. Now Lucia has to find the dogs before their owners return home from work and realize their beloved pets are missing. Lucia knows she won't be paid for losing the dogs. At this point, the goal of her rollerblades seems further away.

All of these problems stand between Lucia and her rollerblades. Though she still wants new rollerblades finding the dogs becomes more important to her.

As you can see from this example, Lucia had a goal of new rollerblades. Unfortunately, she also had external conflict because there was no way of reaching her goal. Lucia came up with a solution, but this solution only creating further obstacles (conflict) that stood between her and new rollerblades.

A problem in fiction can't be too easily solved. The solution creates further obstacles. In other words, the situation gets worse before it gets better and a happy ending is reached.

A character's problem may change and multiply as the story unfolds. In the above example, Lucia's goal changes and becomes that of finding the dogs. However, the original goal should be strong enough to remain until it's eventually resolved at the conclusion of your novel.

How a character reacts to external conflicts depends on her personality, background, strengths and weaknesses. This is why it's so important to know your characters. You must know how they would react when faced with certain obstacles.

If a character reacts in a way that seems contrary to their personality, the character can seem unbelievable to readers. The connection between character and readers is lost. Goodbye readers.

Another person might have stolen the money to buy the rollerblades. Another person might have let the dogs roam free and lied about losing them. Not Lucia. She's a sweet little girl who is responsible and loves animals. She worries that something terrible might happen to the dogs before she can find them.

This story could have gone in several directions depending on the nature of the main character. So, I'll remind you again, characters create the twists and turns in your plots.

Internal Conflict

Internal conflict comes from inside or within a character. It is a struggle that takes place inside the mind of a character and therefore is emotional or psychological. For example, fear, jealousy, phobias, insecurity and envy can cause internal conflict.

Internal conflict sometimes involves a battle between what a character wants to do and what a character must do.

For example, in my novel *Our Secret Place*, a group of boys accidentally burn down an abandoned house they're using as a secret meeting place. Their dilemma is whether to own up or not. They know they should admit their mistake – and it was an accident! But at the same time they don't want to get into trouble and disappoint their parents. They could be fined or, worse, go to jail.

To further compound their dilemma one of the boys has severe burns to his hands as a result of trying to extinguish the flames. He should go to hospital, but refuses because he's afraid the hospital staff will guess the cause of his injuries and ask too many difficult questions.

In the above example, fear, guilt and conscience create internal conflict for the main character and his friends.

How a character reacts to internal conflict depends on his personality, background, strengths and weaknesses. You should know your characters well so you can anticipate how they'll react and what they'll do next.

Wherever possible increase the stakes – up the ante – to make things harder for your characters and, hence, your story more interesting to readers. By upping the ante, you're also upping the care factor. In other words, you elicit more emotion from your readers.

Sometimes I feel mean because I make life as hard as possible for my characters. I do things to them that I wouldn't want to experience myself. I cause them problems I'd rather live without.

A character should learn, grow and change as a result of resolving his conflict, whether it's external or internal. The experiences in your story should change him for the better. Remember that fiction is about escapism. In many ways, we read to make sense of life. Fictional stories are mostly resolved with satisfying endings. Loose ends are neatly tied up. Fictional people learn and become more rounded human beings. Fiction is often an idealized version of the real world.

The way in which a character changes – or, in some cases, refuses to change – is called the character's arc. It's the difference between a mere series of events and a compelling human story. The character's journey from start to end (evolution) of your book is often referred to as the Hero's Journey. These two words give a sense of growth or moving forward.

Readers don't want to see the main character as static or unchanging. What is the point to that? Character growth is part of the satisfaction a reader gains from reading your book.

Moral/Theme

I'm the first to admit that I love a good story for no other reason than the simple fact that it is a good story. It transports me to a different place with different people and different circumstances. This is escapism.

I read for pleasure and entertainment.

A lot of people believe that a children's book should teach children some great lesson about life.

Why? Does an adult book teach adults some great lesson about life?

No. Let's look at an example of adult fiction.

Crime stories might teach us that bad guys always get caught. But is that the author's main goal – to teach us something? Of course not. The author's main goal is to entertain readers with a jolly good yarn.

I can't imagine many authors of crime fiction thinking, "oh, I want to teach people about crime and forensics and most importantly make sure they know that bad guys always get caught so I'll write a crime novel". That's not their major objective. If it was, I'm sure these authors wouldn't write the best possible fictional story. How can they when their focus is not on story, but somewhere else? No, these authors want to write great books readers will enjoy.

If a writer of fictional crime novels really wanted to teach us then her fictional worlds would be more like real life – bad guys don't always get caught, cases are not so neat and tidy and solved in a short space of time. Remember that fiction is an idealized version of reality. If the motivation of a crime writer was to teach then she would most likely write non-fiction books about real criminal cases. Therefore her fictional stories are meant to give readers the pleasure of entertainment and escapism.

Fiction is about characters and story, not lessons about real life. Fiction is fiction.

As writers of children's books, our motivation should be the same – to write great books readers will enjoy.

Make a child read for any reason other than pleasure and entertainment and you risk turning him off books for the rest of his life. The last thing we want is for a child to view books as work or a chore – as teaching.

Now that doesn't mean there can't be a lesson underlying your story.

Sure there can.

However, the lesson, moral or theme should be so subtle that readers don't know it's there. It should be invisible to readers.

A moral or theme should never ever intrude on the story. The story comes first. In other words, entertainment and escapism come first.

Naturally there should be a point to a story. The point is usually related to the character arc or hero's journey. In other words, the character growth and change that takes place by the end of the book. I write my stories first. I write them to entertain readers. I don't think about the moral or lesson until later, if at all.

What is the moral behind *Black Baron?* That all creatures, even cockroaches, deserve our respect. Possibly.

And the lesson behind *The Pony Game?* That we should appreciate our pets and never neglect them. Maybe.

What about my book *Be Careful, Ogre?* That mean people get their just desserts. (I hope so.)

Mr Fix-it, Not! is about accepting people for who they are.

Every reader is different. We're all unique individuals. Therefore, every reader will not get the same message from a book. Readers will interpret a book from their unique perspective and take from a story different meanings. A reader's personality and background come into play.

Another person might think *Mr Fix-it, Not!* is about not trying to fix electrical appliances unless you're good at it. This interpretation is valid, too.

I think you can find some point behind every good story. Otherwise why did the author write it? And why should a child read it?

A story can give us insight into other people's lives. A fictional book could show us what it's like to live in another country. But teaching us something isn't the motivating factor. Story is.

Deliberately setting out to write a moral or lesson is not a good idea.

Never teach or preach to the future leaders of our planet. They can spot these lessons from a mile away and will most likely avoid your books because they feel as if they're being forced to learn, rather than entertained.

Our role, as writers, is to give readers great stories that inspire their interest in books and make them want to keep reading until they gasp their final breaths. That's enough responsibility, thank you very much.

And I suppose, if you really want to get down to it, every children's book teaches problem solving at the very least because the main characters have to face conflict and overcome obstacles on their way to a happy resolution. So there is an added bonus to our stories. Great!

Story is #1

In the section on characters, I told you that stories come from characters and that you can't have stories without characters. Therefore, characters are the most important aspect of any book.

I'm right, of course. (I'm always right!)

Now I'm going to tell you that story is number one. Yes, this does sound like a contradiction, but it isn't.

Once you have a character, and therefore a character's story, story becomes your number one priority and focus.

Think back to the previous section on moral and theme. I told you to never let a moral or theme intrude on a story or you have an excellent chance of losing your readers because people read fiction for pleasure, entertainment and escapism.

To entertain your readers, the story must come first. The story is your number one priority and focus. Your role, as a writer, is to write the best possible story from the best possible characters.

The point here is that you must stick to the story. Don't waffle, don't add unnecessary information, don't go off on tangents – stay on focus, which is the main character's story.

Children's books have limited word lengths. Every word in a children's book – action, dialogue and description – must add to the character's story. If a sentence or paragraph doesn't add to characterization or move the plot forward then you should rewrite it or get rid of it.

In children's books, there is no room for wasted words.

And remember your audience has been raised on a diet of instant gratification – TV, DVDs, computer games etc. You could lose them if you don't stick to the point, if they have to wade through a lot of extra words to find the story.

When I edit a novel I query every sentence. Does the sentence move the plot forward? Does it add to characterization? Is it necessary? Is it repeating an earlier point? If in doubt, I get rid of the sentence. Now how does the section read? Is it better? Worse? Does the paragraph make sense without that sentence?

I often delete a sentence, or more, to be pleasantly surprised at the result. The deletion makes the section stronger and that is my goal.

Writers do have a tendency to repeat themselves, use too many words or unnecessary words, and wander from the point, at least in a first draft. This is one of the reasons you edit your work – to make sure your focus is on the elements necessary to the story.

This focus on story also relates to characters. Does a character move a plot forward? Does she add to the characterization of the main character? Does he add to the conflict? Is this person necessary?

Picture books have few words, in comparison to chapter books or novels. Therefore, every word must be carefully chosen. Writers can spend a lot of time making sure that every word in a picture book does a job and is necessary. These books might look simple and easy, but only because the author has painstakingly considered every word. Less is more in a picture book.

Logic

One of the things I love about children's fiction is the freedom this genre provides for my imagination. I can create futuristic worlds of space cars, flying shopping trolleys and aliens in my book *Martian Milk*. I can invent a small black box that allows a person to transform into another person, animal or object in my book *Mrs Twitch and the Small Black Box*. I can have an Ogre playing hide-and-seek in *Helga and the Ogre*. My writing is only limited by the knowledge and age of my audience.

Children spend a lot of time in the world of make-believe. They have vivid imaginations and are very receptive to fantastic tales.

However, it's important that the worlds we invent and the stories we write are logical. We can write about anything, no matter how fantastic, as long as it makes sense.

It's the writer's job to create worlds where space cars in *Martian Milk* and small black boxes in *Mrs Twitch* are perfectly reasonable and believable.

When I first submitted *Mrs Twitch and the Small Black Box* to a publisher, an editor queried a detail of the plot. The main character changed into an object by pointing the small black box at that object and pressing a button on the box. In the original version of the story, the main character pointed the box at the TV, pressed the button and became her favorite pop star, whose film clip was playing on screen at the time. "Why didn't Jess become the TV?" the editor asked.

The editor wasn't questioning Mrs Twitch's invention – the small black box. She wasn't even questioning Jess' ability to change into other people, animals or objects. She was happy to accept my incredible idea, but for one thing – it didn't make sense to her that Jess became her favorite pop singer and not the TV. And she was right. This detail, though minor, was a logic flaw.

I fixed this problem by adding an extra step to Jess' transformation into an object, person or animal. Jess pointed the small black box at something, pressed the button and wished to be that thing. So, to become the pop star instead of the TV, Jess made that choice through a wish.

I know the story still sounds fantastic. It is. But it's also logical, given the characters and the world I created.

These small details can become huge obstacles to readers' enjoyment of your book. You and your story can too easily lose credibility. Your readers may give up on this novel and all your future works. So it's vital that your stories make sense.

In my novel *Black Baron*, my champion racing cockroach manages to survive two murder attempts. Both attempts are the result of Jake's parents hiring a professional exterminator.

It stretches credibility that *Black Baron* would escape a professional exterminator once, let alone twice – except for one thing.

In the first chapter, I "showed" that *Black Baron* loves hanging out in jacket pockets because he likes warm, dark places. This plot point is no accident. It's vital to credibility. *Black Baron* manages to escape the first time in a jacket pocket. The second time... Well, you'll have to read the book to find out.

This mention, early in the story, of *Black Baron* liking jacket pockets is a clue or hint, known as foreshadowing. I'm foreshadowing something that will come into play later in the story. At this point in the story, the jacket pocket seems unimportant. But, as I mentioned in previous sections, writers should only include what is important or necessary to characterization or the plot. Therefore, foreshadowing the jacket pocket is a subtle hint.

Let your imagination run wild. Write about anything you can imagine. But fantasy must still make sense. It must still be logical. The last thing you want is a reader saying, "Hang on a minute. How come...?"

Lack of logic can ruin an otherwise excellent story.

BACKGROUND

Settings

Settings are necessary. A story has to take place somewhere. However, just as adult characters and morals and themes should never intrude on a children's story, neither should settings.

Picture books are visual, with the illustrations as important as the text. There's no need to describe what's obvious in the illustrations, such as settings. It's clear from the pictures where the story is taking place. You have a limited number of words to work with in picture books. You can't afford to waste them on settings and descriptions that are shown in the illustrations. Naturally the settings in picture books should be familiar to children aged between 4 and 8.

When writing easy readers or transition books, you're still restricted by word length. You don't have a lot of room to describe settings. You don't want to slow the action or detract from the story by including too much detailed description. Only include what is necessary to the plot. Again, it's important to use settings that are familiar to our audience.

In my book *The Pony Game*, the setting is the main character's house. There's something important and unusual about the location of her home that is essential to the story, or it wouldn't work. This next line is the only description of setting included in *The Pony Game* because the book had to be around 2,500 words and, of course, my focus had to be on the character's story.

Lucy lived next door to real stables with real horses.

I didn't have much room to describe setting and there's no need to describe a character's house. Children can imagine a home without the writer's help or interference. This description of setting also added to characterization and moved the plot forward.

As children's books become longer and your audience older, you have more scope for describing setting and including unfamiliar places. In some books, the setting is so important that it almost becomes another character. Most likely the setting is unusual enough to require detailed explanation.

One example is the setting in the novel *Nim's Island* by Wendy Orr. I mention this book because it's now a feature film. The island, Nim's home, is described in detail, including a map, because this information is important to the main character and her story. The setting is unusual and unique in some way. In this case, the story relies heavily on the setting, as does the character. Nim wouldn't be Nim, if she didn't live on this island.

Although my novel *Our Secret Place* is short – between 4,000 and 4,500 words – I spent some time creating a picture of the setting in readers' minds. The following are excerpts from this novel.

> *Weeds brushed damply against our legs as we walked around to the back door.*
> *Apart from oiling the back door to stop it from creaking, we hadn't touched the place. We liked it the way it was – old and dilapidated.*
> *The house was bare. The furniture, curtains and carpets were long gone. The oven, fridge and heaters had disappeared. The only things still there was stuff that couldn't be taken – the walls, floor and roof. Though, in places, the floorboards were missing too.*
> *The broken windows and holes in the wall let in the wind.*

The abandoned house in this novel is essential to the plot, as is the chill of the winter night. Therefore, I included some detail, but I kept it brief because I didn't want to bore readers who are interested in the characters, story and action.

I've read many children's books that mention setting without going into detailed descriptions because the setting isn't important to the plot or not uniquely different to necessitate too much information.

Black Baron takes place in Jake's home and the deli owned by his parents. I mention the rooms Jake and his parents enter or exit, only because their actions around the house are critical to the plot. But I don't bother to describe these rooms or the deli.

Children can create vivid images in their minds of a kitchen or a boy's bedroom, even a deli. I would be describing the obvious and, while doing so, the story would stop. And it's better for readers to use their own ideas of a house and/or deli. Remember that your readers are most interested in the character and his story. What his house looks like is irrelevant, unless, of course, there's something special or unique about it.

A story can have a number of settings. For instance, a children's book can be set in a classroom, school, house, park, backyard etc. The story can move amongst these settings.

However, I mentioned earlier that too many characters and too many plot elements can confuse young children. The same can be said of settings. The younger the audience, the fewer settings you should include in your book.

Writing about setting is akin to painting pictures in readers' minds. You can include things, such as weather, season and time of day, but only if this information is relevant to the character and his story. Otherwise, who cares?

Description

We've already covered a lot of information on description, or lack of it in children's books, so I won't go into too much detail here.

The rule of thumb – never slow a story down with unnecessary description.

Children have vivid imaginations. Give children the opportunity to use their imaginations by minimizing description. You don't need to describe the neighbor's cat further than "black cat". We all know what a black cat looks like. Okay, you might want to add fat or skinny, but nothing more, unless there's something unique about this cat that necessitates extra description.

In a 2,500 word illustrated story, such as my book *The Pony Game*, you don't need descriptions of your characters, their homes and furniture. Firstly, you don't have enough words to spare. Secondly, the illustrations are there for the looking, even if they're black and white.

Description in *The Pony Game* is limited to a horse, Midnight, the main character looks after for a week and only because of the main character's reaction to it, which is integral to the plot. The humans are not described, nor are the house, back yard or stables (settings).

Jake's appearance isn't described in *Black Baron*, a novel of approximately 10,000 words. I show his personality through dialogue, actions and thoughts, allowing readers to get an impression of him and work the rest out for themselves.

Readers don't want you, the writer, to do all the work for them.

Why are they reading your book?

To use their imaginations and end up with an enjoyable period of escapism, right?

Your readers don't want you describing everything for them. Then there's nothing for them to bring to the story, nothing for them to do. They could become bored with your novel and do something else.

Research

Sometimes it's necessary to research an aspect (or aspects) of your story, such as a setting or period in time.

Research is different from a character biography or character development, though your research might add to characterization.

Let's say you wanted to write a novel about a boy who goes on a dig to excavate dinosaur fossils and gets caught up in a mystery involving theft and smuggling. Unless you already know about these kinds of digs, dinosaurs and fossils, then you'll have to research the subjects so you can write a convincing believable story. Some of the information gained will help in developing your main character. One would assume he's interested in fossils for starters. If not, then you have a different story.

For example, my book *Caught in a Cyclone* is about a family caught in Cyclone Tracy which devastated Darwin, in Northern Territory, Australia, on Christmas Eve 1974. In other words, the story is based on a real event. I remember, as a child, seeing the news of the cyclone on television and the recordings of the widespread devastation. But I wasn't there and I knew little of the details, let alone what it's like to live through a major cyclone.

To write *Caught in a Cyclone* I had to do a lot of research. I had to know when and how the cyclone occurred, and why it caused such havoc. I had to learn the time frame of events, accompanying weather conditions and damage. I also had to know something about the setting of Darwin and types of homes, plus remain faithful to the period.

If I didn't do my research, my lack of knowledge or guesswork could be obvious to readers, especially people living in Darwin at the time of Cyclone Tracy. Even the smallest of mistakes reduces readers' enjoyment of your story, gives readers an excuse to stop reading and harms your credibility. Chances are they would never pick up one of your stories again.

My research paid off. Several people have asked me if I was living in Darwin and experienced Cyclone Tracy. Well, yes, but only fictionally 20 years later.

Writers are often told to write about what they know. I think this is good advice for new writers. Sticking to what you know reduces the chances of errors creeping into your novel. And starting your career with a story that needs a lot of research is just making life harder for you.

However, I wouldn't limit yourself for the remainder of your writing career. Writing about unfamiliar topics can work well as long as you do your homework. If in doubt, always check your facts. Even if you're certain about something, it still pays to check your facts.

When researching a story, you should always end up with a lot more information than eventually appears in your novel. Only include what is necessary. Information, like description, should never slow a story down. It should always add to a story. That is, it should move the plot forward, add to characterization or conflict.

Necessary information that you have to include in your story should never look like necessary information that you have to include your story. It should be restricted to short descriptions, preferably from the main character's point of view, or conveyed through dialogue, feelings or thoughts, so as to keep the story moving and keep the reader interested. Remember the character's story is number one. Always focus on the character and how things affect her, what she's doing, feeling, thinking and experiencing.

Few people want to read a book, to escape the drudgery of everyday life, and be lectured on the kind of armor used by Sir Whatshisfoot in whatever century. But if this information is sprinkled into the story, from the main character's point of view or another character's point of view, then we're only too happy to read about it if it's relevant to the story.

One day, a successful children's author told me that she preferred writing fantasy to reality-based fiction because readers are less likely to pick fault with her stories. They are less judgmental and critical about her imagined worlds and fantastic plot lines.

I write both fantasy and reality-based fiction. I don't have a preference. I'm simply writing a character's story.

No matter what you choose to write, your story must always be accurate, credible and logical.

Five Senses

In any kind of fictional writing you should remember the five senses. Where possible use these senses to add power to your descriptions and thus, add to believability.

Yes, the shorter word length of children's fiction has its limitations. But, where possible, remembering to use the five senses will improve the quality of your writing.

When we use the five senses, we show (don't tell) readers what is happening in a scene. We give them the opportunity to fully experience our fictitious world through their own senses. Of course, this is the way we experience the real world.

The important thing to remember here is relevance to the plot. If you simply add some reference to the smell of roses or the sound of buzzing bees and they have no relevance to the plot, you're wasting words and slowing down the story. Your readers aren't interested in the smell of roses or the sound of buzzing bees. They're interested in your character's story.

There were opportunities for me to use the five senses in my novel Our Secret Place. In fact, given the story features a house fire on a winter evening, not using at least some of the five senses could be considered bad writing. Here are a few examples from *Our Secret Place:*

> *All that bare wood and fire were an explosive combination – a fireball. Orange flames leapt into the black sky.* (Sight) *The house crackled and popped like breakfast cereal.* (Sound) *Heat radiated from the flames, warming the winter air.* (Touch)
>
> *The street was soon filled with people, as though the houses had suddenly tossed their contents all over the street. I heard sirens in the distance.* (Sound) *Then, minutes later, I saw the flashing red lights of two fire engines.* (Sight)

Description is kept to a minimum, but still includes the senses, as should any good fire story.

Take care when selecting your words. The right word can inspire more than one of the senses. For example, from *Our Secret Place:*

> *All that was left of our secret meeting place was a smoldering shell.*

To me, the word smoldering inspires two of my senses, sight and smell.

These descriptions make the fire come alive for my readers to fully experience.

Yes, do limit your description, but when you do describe something because it's important to the story make the description vibrant and sensual.

When you use description, similes and metaphors in children's fiction you have to remember your audience. Children must be able to relate to your writing. Pick words and phrases that children would use, that are familiar to their worlds. Sometimes new writers let adult phrases, similes, metaphors or ideas creep into their writing. New writers are familiar with these words, sayings or phrases that are common in adult conversation, and use them automatically without thinking.

OTHER THINGS TO CONSIDER

Openings

If you have read books about writing, you would have discovered a lot of talk about opening pages, opening paragraphs and even opening sentences.

A writer has to grab their readers in the opening chapter. Yes, this is true.

However, children have a lot to do. They can do their homework. Heaven forbid that homework is more enjoyable than your book! They can play with friends. They can play sport or computer games. They can hang out at the mall or go shopping. They can surf the Internet.

Children have shorter attention spans than adults. It's more important to grab them early in a book and keep them hooked. We don't want them losing interest and going to play a video game or watch TV.

Grab them in the first sentence.

This is the first sentence from *Our Secret Place:*

> *"I'm going out," I said.*

Okay, so that isn't the most exciting sentence ever written. It won't win any awards. But it does one thing. It makes you curious. Who is going out? Where is he going? Why is he going? Should we even care?

Readers want to know more. And that's the whole idea. It's the writer's job to make readers want to read their book, from the first line to the last.

Hook readers in the first sentence and keep them hooked.

Here are the next five lines from *Our Secret Place:*

> *"Where?" Mom asked.*
> *"Luke's house," I said.*
> *"Don't forget your coat."*
> *I put on my jacket. Not because Mom told me to, but because it was freezing where I was headed.*

I don't know about you, but I suspect the main character isn't going to Luke's house – because it's freezing where he's headed. So where is he going? And why is he lying to his mother?

The suspicion is soon confirmed.

> *At the top of the drive, I turned left. This was not the way to Luke's house. I wasn't going to Luke's house. I was meeting my mates at our secret meeting place…*

Children's books always start in the middle of the action. By the end of the first chapter, your reader should have met the main character and be aware of his internal or external conflict. The sooner you can introduce this information the better. The first few pages should be your goal.

Here are the first few sentences of *Black Baron.*

> *"Go, Black Baron!" I yelled.*
> *The Baron raced across the concrete. He was almost home. We were almost champions. Again!*

Then he stopped. My heart hit my shoes. Bugsy was catching up.

In the first page, the reader has met the main character, learned about his participation in cockroach racing and been introduced to the champion Black Baron. The reader is in the middle of the action. By the end of the chapter readers know the problem or external conflict.

Here are the closing sentences of the first chapter of *Black Baron*:

I should have taken Black Baron with me. I would have taken him with me if I'd known he was in danger.
If only I'd kept my promise.

Another reason for writing a beginning that hooks readers is the purely practical business of interesting an agent or publisher in your book. Given the number of submissions agents and publishers receive, they often only read the first page or so of a manuscript before making a decision to continue reading or return the submission to the writer with a rejection letter or slip. Therefore, it's vital that your story inspires an agent or publisher to keep reading. Publishing is a professional industry and these personnel make a decision about your story, based on their experience, almost immediately.

The first few lines of any novel are the hardest to write and the ones that will probably take the most time. The next most demanding and challenging is the ending.

Endings

I mentioned earlier in this book that fiction for children up to about 13 years old (pre-young adult) always has a happy ending.

Your main character and her actions should bring about the resolution to the story. She can have assistance from friends and family. However, she should always be the main catalyst for resolving her problems/conflict and reaching her goal.

Imagine the disappointment for readers if they've followed a character through a novel only to have someone else step in at the last moment and fix everything. Especially as children read for escapism, and that includes gaining feelings of maturity, independence and power. One of the last things they want is to lose this sense of maturity, independence and power at the end of your book because someone else, other than the main character readers are identifying with, has came to the rescue.

Never leave any loose ends. You should fix every problem and answer every question, all in the goal of satisfying your readers. A flat or unresolved ending can easily ruin a good story.

Children like routine, order and discipline, even though they might not realize it and may act to the contrary. A nicely constructed ending that resolves everything for readers fits children's need for structure and order.

The major studios in Hollywood understand this desire for resolution. The reason most Hollywood movies finish with a happy ending that makes us feel good and neatly resolves all issues and questions is because it's what the public wants. Apparently humans desire resolution and closure, order and structure, which is often contrary to life on planet Earth. Hollywood gives us all these things in carefully constructed stories on the screen. As a screenwriter, I've discovered there's a formula for Hollywood movies. These stories are very deliberately and precisely created so we keep coming back for more.

Once the resolution has been reached, with all the loose ends nicely stitched up, the story should finish quickly. It's tempting for some writers to show life has returned to normal or improved for the main character, but this is unnecessary and reduces the satisfaction of the ending.

I like to know the ending before I start writing a story. Knowing the ending gives me a direction to head in, something to aim for, and I feel more confident about finishing the story. It also allows me to prepare readers for my ending. I can drop clues into the story or foreshadow events, so the ending seems perfectly logical and satisfactory, as if there was no other way for the story to finish. Mysteries are a perfect example of having to place clues and foreshadow events.

Black Baron has a surprise ending. Readers don't expect the final scenes, yet they make sense given the characters and the story. I'd love to tell you about the ending, but that would spoil the book for you.

Whatever the ending, it must be satisfying.

Chapters

Baby books and picture books do not have chapters. Easy readers and transition books often have chapters, but it depends on the publisher's guidelines. Obviously, all children's books have chapters once you reach the word length of chapter books.

So what is the purpose of chapters?

Chapters break stories into manageable chunks. This is important to child readers. The appearance of pages and pages and pages of text to a young person learning to read can be enough to put them off books for life. Children are reluctant to pursue anything that looks too difficult. (Aren't we all!)

For the same reason, paragraphs are usually short in these early children's books. The appearance of plenty of white space on the pages is deliberate because it's attractive and reassuring to young readers.

Chapters give young readers the sense of reading "grown up" books. They've graduated from picture books to chapter books, which are similar in appearance to the novels their parents read.

Chapters often mean transitions in time and/or settings. We readily accept that it's now next week or the character is at school because we've finished one chapter and moved on to the next. Time or location has changed, indicated by a chapter break.

The chapter can be a writer's best friend. How many of you have read books where you come to the end of one chapter and you have to keep reading because you want to know what happens next, you need to know what happens next?

A chapter is similar to the season finale of your favorite soap opera or television series. You're faced with a cliffhanger and you can hardly wait until the next episode next season to see what happens.

At the end of every chapter, I aim to give my readers a mini cliffhanger. I want them to keep reading, to be unable to put my book down. This might not eventuate in my first draft, but during the editing process I take extra time with my chapter endings and look for the right one, the right sentence that makes it impossible for readers to leave my character and story.

Sure, chapters are supposed to be a good place to stop in a story, but my goal, as a writer, is to make readers want to keep reading. I haven't worked hard enough if they can easily put down my book.

To show you what I mean, here are two chapter endings from my novel *Backstage Betrayal*. After rehearsal for the school play, Laura is locked in the old theatre when everyone else goes home.

Ending of Chapter Two:

... Like a wild animal taking flight, Laura leaps for the outer door and pulls at the handle.
    The door doesn't budge.

Readers realize that Laura is locked in the toilet. Will she be able to get out? Or will she have to stay there? For how long? The only way to know what's going to happen is to continue reading the book.

Ending of Chapter Three:

> ...*Or the windows high up in the wall?*
> *Windows!*
> *Smiling, Laura plans her great escape.*

What great escape? Will she make it? The only way to find out is to continue reading the book.

Here is the Chapter Two ending from *The Pony Game:*

> *In her excitement, Lucy had forgotten her parents. What would they think about her going to the stables? She hoped they would agree to her taking care of Midnight. They had to agree.*

Posing a question is a good way to create a cliffhanger. In the above example from *The Pony Game*, the main character wonders what her parents will think and then makes her own desires clear. End of chapter. Readers have to read on to find out what the parents will do and therefore what happens next, all of which is related to the main character's goal. Will she or won't she?

Subplots

There is no room for subplots in baby books, picture books, easy readers or transition books. The word length is simply too short and the audience is too young to follow complicated plots.

What is a subplot?

A subplot is a smaller story within a larger main story. If you imagine your main plot is story "A", then a subplot would be story "B" or, with more than one subplot, stories "B" and "C".

A subplot is always smaller than the main story and therefore takes up less room/action. It's also less important. The job of a subplot is to enhance the main story.

A novel can have several subplots, but in children's books it's best to keep subplots to a minimum. Most stories, even adult novels, can only support one to three subplots.

Why do we need subplots?

Subplots in longer children's books add interest and another layer to a story. They reflect real life where more than one thing happens at a time. No one story happens in isolation.

Subplots add to the main story in some way – move it along by adding to conflict, theme or characterization. A subplot should never change the main plot, but it can affect the main story and alter the course of it.

A subplot should never be a filler to add to the word length. It should always have some connection to the main story, some relevance. This is especially important in children's fiction where every word has to work hard due to the limited word length.

A subplot should never become more important than the main story. Otherwise, you're writing the wrong story. It's time for a rewrite.

Subplots can be resolved at any time during your novel. Remember that the end of your novel must resolve all loose ends, including subplots. Therefore, each subplot is structured as a complete story within or connected to another larger story.

In my book, *Stop! Do Not Read This Book*, I included a subplot about Troy's dog. Hound has a humungous farting problem. The subplot adds light relief to a story that focuses on a serious problem. But humor by itself is not enough reason to include a subplot. In this example, Hound's problem also adds to the main plot.

Troy takes Hound to see a specialist in the hope of curing his pet's embarrassing farting problem. A school friend sees Troy leaving the specialist's office and assumes Troy is the patient. This mix-up causes Troy embarrassment and makes the final resolution of the novel seem further away.

You can see that this subplot moves the plot forward. That is, it causes further complications for the main character when he thinks a resolution is near. The subplot is introduced in the first few pages of the story, but doesn't become a plot obstacle for Troy until near the end of the book.

A second subplot in this story is a romantic interest for Troy. Troy is trying to impress Jo. Near the climax of the story it appears that Troy has not only failed, but has done the opposite. At the end of the story it's clear that Jo feels the same way about Troy.

This subplot is connected to the main story because many of the obstacles that face the main character have an impact on this budding romance.

THE FINAL COUNTDOWN

Editing Tips

The first point I want to make about editing is to delay it. I'm not encouraging procrastination. Far from it! Before you start editing, ideally you should put your completed manuscript away for as long as possible – a minimum of one week, longer if practical. When you're working on a story you're too close to it to see the errors and required improvements. By putting your manuscript away for an extended period you're trying to create some distance from it, thereby making it easier to see the necessary editorial changes.

When you think your novel is finished – after several rewrites and edits on screen –print the manuscript out. It's much easier to edit on a hard copy than it is on your computer. There's something about words on paper that make problems in a manuscript much easier to identify.

Your manuscript should be double-spaced with wide margins, allowing you plenty of white space for scribbled notes or changes.

Using a pencil allows you to make temporary marks and alterations on your manuscript that can be rubbed out later if you change your mind. Deleting or altering text on a computer can be frighteningly final.

Now, sit down in a quiet place with your manuscript, pencil and your characters' biographies. You need undisturbed time for as long as possible to complete the editing process. Pull out the telephone plug or turn on the answering machine. Don't answer the door. Hire a babysitter. Send your husband or wife out to play golf. Do whatever it takes to ensure you have long periods of quiet time.

The reason I have my characters' biographies handy is so I can check every detail for consistency – the characters' appearances, habits, families, homes etc. If you've accidentally changed the main character's eye color, for example, at some point during the writing of your manuscript, you want to find the error now, during editing.

When editing a shorter novel, I ask my partner to read my manuscript to me. If he stumbles on a word or sentence I know there's a problem that needs addressing. I ask him to mark the spot then continue reading. As I listen, if anything bothers me, I ask him to mark the spot. Afterwards, I return to the marked spots and revise. Reading out loud slows your reading down and allows you to think about every word and image. It also allows you to hear any sentence, phrase or word readers might stumble on.

It's best to edit your manuscript in one sitting to keep you in touch with the flow of the story. Flow is one of the things you're checking during the editing process.

Sometimes improvements to sentences or paragraphs are immediately apparent. Sometimes they are not.

If the improvement is immediately apparent, i.e. the option of using a better word, such as "returned" instead of "went back", I make a note on the manuscript. If the improvement is not apparent, I mark the sentence with a cross. This tells me to return to the sentence later and rework it. I don't want to get bogged down with heavy rewrites during this editing process as it disturbs the flow of the story.

I have returned to a sentence later and puzzled over why I marked it with a cross. It seems fine. I guess it depends on my mood at the time – maybe I was being too fussy.

I always read my stories out loud. I stop and question every sentence. This takes many hours, but it's worth it in the end because the result is a much tighter story.

What do I look for when I'm doing a line edit (in no particular order)?

a) *Flow*

b) *Smooth transitions between sentences and/or paragraphs*

c) *Repetition*

d) *Sloppy sentences or lazy writing*

e) *Unnecessary words or sentences*

f) *Wordiness*

g) *Stating the obvious*

h) *Clarity in meaning*

i) *Additions to make a scene better or clearer*

j) *Deletions to make a scene better or clearer*

k) *Weak sentences or sentences that end on a weak word*

l) *Logic*

m) *Inaccuracy*

n) *Inconsistency with characters and their behavior*

o) *Clichés*

During editing, I check to ensure every chapter finishes with a page-turner (cliffhanger). If one doesn't, I scribble notes in the margin or mark the last sentence with a cross.

Sometimes it's necessary for writers to delete what we consider to be fine writing – a sentence or section we're particularly proud of and attached to. There's a saying "murder your darlings". Yes, there are times when you do have to delete some of your favorite lines of writing to improve the overall story.

It doesn't matter how good a section is if it doesn't add to the plot in some way – move the story forward or add to characterization, conflict or theme – we have no choice but to delete it. Sometimes it's hard to part with these fine pieces of writing.

Everyone works differently, and we have to do what works for us. The above are simply things that work for me. They may work for you. You may have better techniques.

Publishers and the Market

So, your baby (manuscript) is ready to take its first step into the big, wide world of publishing. Congratulations. Writing a novel is a huge achievement. You should be proud of yourself. Well done!

Where do you plan to send your manuscript?

If you don't already know the answer now is the time to research the market.

Do you have access to a writers' reference book on market places?

For example, *Writer's Market* is published by *Writer's Digest* in the US, *Writers' and Artists' Yearbook* is published by A & C Black in the UK and *The Australian Writer's Marketplace* is published by the Queensland Writers' Centre in Australia.

These reference guides list the various markets important to writers. They list book publishers as well as magazines, competitions, agents, writers' centers and more. Included in the publisher information are contact details, what they publish, if they accept unsolicited manuscripts and their submission guidelines.

Unfortunately, replacing these books every year is an expensive proposition. Try borrowing them from a friend or your local library. Nowadays it's possible to access these reference guides online, usually by paying a subscription.

Another way of discovering this information is by visiting publishers' websites. You can also telephone or email publishers and ask for their guidelines, if they aren't already available online.

It's an excellent idea to visit a good bookstore that stocks a wide range of children's books. Have a look at the types of books being published and who is publishing them. Find books that are similar to yours in length and target audience.

Looking at books in a bookstore also gives you an idea of what series are being published. But remember that it takes approximately 18 months for a book to land on a bookstore's shelf. What the publisher wanted 18 months ago could be different from what they want today. Do not send your children's book to a publisher that only publishes travel books.

Do not send your children's book to a publisher that only publishes fiction and non-fiction for adults.

Do not send your young adult novel about drug abuse to a publisher who publishes religious fiction.

Some publishers do not accept unsolicited manuscripts. Their books are commissioned or they only consider manuscripts recommended by agents.

When a publisher has a great backlog of unsolicited manuscripts, to allow them to catch up, they may temporarily close their doors to unsolicited submissions.

Some publishers only accept unsolicited manuscripts that have been professionally assessed by an assessment agency.

You can save time and money, and reduce disappointment, by doing your homework. Research the market before you submit your manuscript and target the most likely publishers first.

Submitting Your Manuscript

How does your manuscript look?

I'm not interested in the story now. I'm only interested in the appearance of the manuscript and how you've formatted it.

The following is the standard when submitting your manuscript to a publisher:

a)   *Clean, white paper.*

b)   *Easy to read font, most commonly Times New Roman.*

c)   *Double-spaced with margins of 3cms or one inch on both sides.*

d)   *Dark print and printed on one side of the paper only.*

e)   *Indent the beginning of each paragraph.*

f)   *Justify the left margin only.*

g)   *Page number on every page.*

h)   *Your name or the title of the manuscript on every page.*

Your manuscript should also be free of typos, errors or evidence of corrected errors.

The title page should include:

a)   Title of your story.

b)   Your contact details – name, address, telephone and fax numbers, mobile and email address.

c)   Word count.

d)   Age of target audience.

Never send a hand-written story to a publisher.

Sure, a picture book is short. Why go to the trouble of typing it on a computer?

If you want to be published you had better type it on a computer for two reasons:

a)   So the poor publisher, who has eyestrain from reading too many manuscripts, can read your submission.

b)   You want to look like a professional writer, not someone who threw a story together in five minutes.

Most publishers will tell you to submit your manuscript to the Children's Editor or Senior Editor or some similar title. You could go to the trouble of telephoning the publisher to find out the person's name. A personally addressed submission might help. However, I've telephoned publishers and asked for the name of the Children's Editor, only to be told to just send the manuscript to the Children's Editor.

You should always check a publisher's guidelines before submitting your manuscript. But, typically, your submission should include:

a)   A covering letter.

b)   A writer's biography (CV).

c)   A synopsis of your novel – no more than two/three double-spaced pages.

d)   The first three chapters of your novel.

e)   A stamped self-addressed envelope large enough for return of your manuscript or a business-sized letter.

If you don't want your manuscript returned to you – to save money on postage – you must tell the publisher in your covering letter and include a business-sized stamped self-addressed envelope for their response to your submission.

If you're submitting a picture book you can enclose the entire manuscript and forget the synopsis. A synopsis for a picture book would be almost the same length as the manuscript. It's unnecessary.

Waiting for a publisher's response to your submission requires a great deal of patience. Most publishers take a minimum of 3 months to respond, but 6 months seems to be the norm nowadays.

As a result, most publishers accept multiple submissions. A multiple submission means that you, the writer, can submit your manuscript to multiple publishers at the same time. In other words, you can send your submission to more than one publisher. You should tell a publisher in your covering letter if you're sending a multiple submission.

Some publishers will not accept multiple submissions. Their guidelines state single submission. The publisher wants to be the only one considering your manuscript at a given time. They don't want to spend time on your submission to have it accepted by another publisher.

Always check a publisher's guidelines to see if they will consider a multiple submission.

Publishers receive thousands of unsolicited manuscripts a year. Some publishers receive thousands of unsolicited manuscripts a week. Give your submission the best possible chance by following the guidelines and thus, appearing professional.

Resources and Courses

One day, I decided I wanted to write children's books with the goal of becoming a published author. Approximately five years later, I reached my goal and my first three books were published. I often refer to these five years as my apprenticeship. I spent this time reading books about writing for children, completing relevant courses, attending seminars and writing in every spare moment. I did everything I could to improve my writing skills, learn about the industry and give myself the best chance of being published.

Children's fiction is different from adult fiction. When you read books about writing choose those that are specific to children's fiction. The same is true of writing courses. You need to learn about writing for children if this is your genre of choice.

After gaining some knowledge from books and practice from writing my own stories, I completed a course on writing children's books conducted by a local university. Three of the stories I wrote for this course were published in 2000.

Find out what courses you can do online or in your own area. Do the local colleges, writers' centers or adult education facilities conduct courses on writing for children?

Join your local writers' center or writing groups. You can also join writers' groups or forums on the Internet for people interested in writing for children.

Make friends with people who share your interest in writing children's books. They can live in your town or you can correspond by email.

In December 2007, during my blog tour for *The Pony Game*, I was asked the question – what is the most important piece of advice you can give prospective writers? As we're nearing the end of this book, I'll repeat my answer here:

"I think the most important advice is to learn about writing for children and to learn from people who are in the industry. That means reading books on the subject, doing courses and getting feedback from experienced children's authors. All of this hones people's writing skills and helps them write stories that fit the market, even if they aren't quite ready for publication. I always recommend manuscript assessments before sending anything to a publisher or publishers. I think feedback from other writers, with experience, is invaluable. It worked for me, pointed out my strengths and weaknesses. I needed to know my weaknesses so I could improve. Networking is another factor which I think is very important. All of my opportunities have come from networking with people in the industry."

IN CLOSING

Common Problems

As the coordinator of a writers' group for unpublished writers of children's books, I've met a lot of would-be writers. I've also seen a lot of manuscripts through the writers' group, tutoring online and, more recently, as a judge of a new writers' contest.

There are a number of common mistakes novice writers make when writing their first children's books:

a)   *The idea that writing children's fiction is easy.*

b)   *Not bothering to learn about children's fiction and undertake writing courses.*

c)   *Using language and a voice that is too grown up for this audience.*

d)   *Writing from the point of view of an adult author, not from the point of view of a child main character.*

e)   *Authorial intrusion (which relates to the point above).*

f)   *Switching points of view.*

g)   *Telling, instead of showing.*

We've already discussed these problems at length. I point them out here to indicate that they're the most common problems I've discovered in manuscripts written by new writers.

Be aware of these problems and eliminate them from your manuscripts before you submit to publishers.

The 3 Ps

So what are the three Ps?

Practice

It doesn't matter what profession you enter, everyone has to learn the trade. People are shown what to do, they do it, and only through practice do they become accomplished at a profession.

Writing is no different.

Writing is a profession. You must learn your trade. You must practice, practice and practice to improve your skills.

Sure, we can all sit down and write. We were taught how to write many years ago when we were tiny tots. But writing for a living is a totally different matter.

Very few people sit down, write a first book and get it published. Most writers hone their skills on a number of unpublished works before they score their first contract with a publisher. And this process can take years. Also, there's a big difference between a good story and a publishable story. Knowledge of the industry will help you realize how to write a book that fits somewhere in the marketplace.

A lot of successful authors are embarrassed by their first works – even their first published novels. We all get better over time. Practice makes us better writers. We will never be perfect. Human beings are not perfect creatures. But we can strive to improve by learning as much about our craft as possible and by practicing. Our writing becomes tighter. We write better quality first drafts.

You'll notice the change – over time. I did!

Patience

Patience is an important trait for any writer.

It takes time to write a novel. It takes even more time to write, rewrite and edit your best possible draft of that novel. You can't take short cuts. You can't compromise the quality of your writing – if you want it to be published. You have to stick with a job until it's done to the best of your ability.

It also takes time to hear a response from a publisher after you submit your manuscript. You have to wait a minimum of three months, usually longer. Don't be tempted to pester a publisher to hurry their decision on your submission. They could reject it just to get rid of you.

A polite enquiry is fine, but only after three months and never too often. You don't want to annoy a publisher to the point that they decide they don't want to work with you, even if your story is a potential best-seller.

Once your manuscript has been contracted by a publisher it will probably take one to two years before you see your baby in print. There's no rushing this process. It takes time and a publisher has to fit your book into their publishing program when it suits them, not you. This is a business and publishers plan their lists well in advance. Most publishing lists will be full for this year and often the next year. Your book slots in somewhere in the future, maybe 18 to 24 months away.

You have to learn the art of patience. As a writer, you simply have no choice.

Persistence

I've spoken to a lot of writers and read about many others. Most of them say that the secret to their success is persistence. They never gave up. Of course they could be being modest, but persistence does seem to be the common thread.

Most writers have received numerous rejections. I heard one say that he could wallpaper his office with rejections. But these writers had faith in themselves and their work. They kept on submitting. They kept on writing.

Apparently 28 publishers rejected the first *Dr Seuss'* book.

The first *Harry Potter* novel was rejected by at least three (some say many more) publishers before it was accepted by Bloomsbury.

Publishers rejected *Possum Magic* by Mem Fox nine times in five years, but this went on to become a best-selling children's book in Australia, with more than one million copies sold. Last year commemorated the twenty-five anniversary.

Even a mystery written by Enid Blyton was rejected by her publisher at the height of her fame.

I've received too many rejections. However, I have 89 published titles because I persisted. This is the key to my success – never giving up.

Type the key words "children's author" and "rejected" into a Google search. I'm sure the number of rejections many published authors have received will surprise you. I just did this exercise. Interesting!

Regardless of the industry – television, movies, sport, the business world – successful people work hard and persevere.

Most rejection letters are a standard form letter sent by publishers who simply don't have time for personal comments or feedback. If you do receive a hand-written note or personal letter from a publisher you can take it as a HUGE compliment – the publisher believes you will publish with them or another publisher one day.

Don't take rejection personally. Your manuscript may be rejected for any number of reasons that have nothing to do with the quality of your work.

Some reasons for rejection:

a)   *The publisher's list is full for the next 18 months.*

b)   *The publisher has recently accepted another book with the same theme.*

c)   *The publisher has recently accepted another dog, cat, budgie or similar book.*

d)   *The publisher may have too many unsolicited manuscripts.*

e)   *You haven't properly targeted your manuscript to the right publisher.*

f)   *An editor may be in a bad mood (though he would probably never admit this one).*

However, if too many publishers reject your manuscript then it's time to sit down, rethink and rework it, or start on something new. There may be some problems with your story, characters etc.

Happy writing!

Robyn

ROBYN OPIE PARNELL'S BOOKS

Jen Stays Inside (Macmillan Education, 1999)

My Bike (Macmillan Education, 1999)

People Need Trucks (Macmillan Education, 1999)

Working like a Dog (Macmillan Education, 1999)

The Mad Mower (Macmillan Education, 1999)

Mrs Twitch and the Small Black Box (Macmillan, 1999)

Jack's Great Search (Macmillan Education, 2000)

Martian Milk (Macmillan Education, 2000)

The Mad Mower (Troll, 2000)

My Bike (Troll, 2000)

Working Like a Dog (Troll, 2000)

Living in Space (ETA Cuisenaire, 2001)

Will You Play? (ETA Cuisenaire, 2002)

Ben's Colours (ETA Cuisenaire, 2002)

Ben and the Cold (ETA Cuisenaire, 2002)

Looking After a Dog (ETA Cuisenaire, 2002)

Running (ETA Cuisenaire, 2002)

I Can Ride (ETA Cuisenaire, 2002)

I Am Jumping (ETA Cuisenaire, 2002)

I Am Going (ETA Cuisenaire, 2002)

Jo and the Spider (ETA Cuisenaire, 2002)

Anna's Big Day (ETA Cuisenaire, 2002)

Leafy Sea-dragons (ETA Cuisenaire, 2002)

Where a Cat Sleeps (Soluny, 2002)

Day and Night (Soluny, 2002)

The Wig (Soluny, 2002)

Our Secret Place (Blake Education, 2002)

Backstage Betrayal (Blake Education, 2002)

Five Senses (ETA Cuisenaire, 2002)

What Am I? (ETA Cuisenaire, 2002)

I Could Be (ETA Cuisenaire, 2002)

Feeding (ETA Cuisenaire, 2002)

I Can Draw (ETA Cuisenaire, 2002)

Potato Printing (ETA Cuisenaire, 2002)

The Other Side (ETA Cuisenaire, 2002)

Visiting the Vet (ETA Cuisenaire, 2002)

Making Ice Cream (ETA Cuisenaire, 2003)

The Bell on the Cat (ETA Cuisenaire, 2003)

Ben and the Crab (ETA Cuisenaire, 2003)

Down the Well (ETA Cuisenaire, 2003)

Eye of the Future (Blake Education, 2003)

Old Teddy (ETA Cuisenaire, 2003)

Sam's Dinosaur Bone (ETA Cuisenaire, 2003)

Animal Shelters (ETA Cuisenaire, 2003)

Sea Stars (ETA Cuisenaire, 2003)

Cuttlebone (ETA Cuisenaire, 2003)

Be Careful, Ogre! (ETA Cuisenaire, 2003)

Chick Catches Dinner (ETA Cuisenaire, 2003)

Helga and the Ogre (ETA Cuisenaire, 2004)

A Magnifying Glass (ETA Cuisenaire, 2004)

Good Fires, Bad Fires (ETA Cuisenaire, 2004)

Fire Fighters (ETA Cuisenaire, 2004)

Alice's Funny Photo (ETA Cuisenaire, 2004)

Teddy's Sticky Mess (ETA Cuisenaire, 2004)

Octopus, Cuttlefish & Squid (ETA Cuisenaire, 2004)

How to Write a Great Picture Book (Robyn Opie, 2004)

Furniture (ETA Cuisenaire, 2005)

Getting to Grandma (ETA Cuisenaire, 2005)

The Key (ETA Cuisenaire, 2005)

The Haircut (ETA Cuisenaire, 2005)

Making Gingerbread People (ETA Cuisenaire, 2005)

Sea Animals to Avoid (ETA Cuisenaire, 2005)

Harry and Gran (ETA Cuisenaire, 2005)

Don't Break the Eggs (ETA Cuisenaire, 2005)

Show, Don't Tell Study Pack (Robyn Opie, 2006)

The Pony Game (Lothian Books, 2007)

Backstage Betrayal (Steck Vaughn, 2007)

Our Secret Place (Steck Vaughn, 2007)

Mr Fix-it, Not! (Gan Aschehoug, 2008)

Caught in a Cyclone (Gan Aschehoug, 2008)

Fox Meets Shark (ETA Cuisenaire, 2008)

Fox Meets Shark (Gan Aschehoug, 2008)

Mr Fix-it, Not! (Gan Aschehoug, 2008)

Caught in a Cyclone (Gan Aschehoug, 2008)

Child Heroes: Iqbal Masih (Gan Aschehoug, 2008)

The Seven Continents (Gan Aschehoug, 2008)

Why Was It Built? (Gan Aschehoug, 2008)

Black Baron (Walker Books Australia, 2008)

Little Red Hen (Adastra Laromedel, 2008)

Black Baron (Walker Books UK, 2009)

How to Write a Great Children's Book (Magellan Books, 2010)

Maya and the Crystal Skull (R & R Books Film Music, 2011)

Caught in a Cyclone (R & R Books Film Music, 2011)

Stop! Do Not Read This Book (R & R Books Film Music, 2012)

Best Joke Ever (R & R Books Film Music, 2012)

You're Amazing (R & R Books Film Music, 2012)

Maya and the Daring Heist (R & R Books Film Music, 2013)

28823382R00078

Made in the USA
San Bernardino, CA
07 January 2016